THE QUEST for CHRIST

Discipling Today's Young Adults

Flagship church resources

from Group Publishing

Innovations From Leading Churches

Flagship Church Resources are your shortcut to innovative and effective leadership ideas. You'll find ideas for every area of church leadership including pastoral ministry, adult ministry, youth ministry, and children's ministry.

Flagship Church Resources are created by the leaders of thriving, dynamic, and trend-setting churches around the country. These nationally recognized teaching churches host regional leadership conferences and are respected by other pastors and church leaders because their approaches to ministry are so effective. These flagship church resources reveal the proven ideas, programs, and principles that these churches have put into practice.

Flagship Church Resources currently available:

- *60 Simple Secrets Every Pastor Should Know*
- *The Perfectly Imperfect Church: Redefining the "Ideal Church"*
- *The Winning Spirit: Empowering Teenagers Through God's Grace*
- *Ultimate Skits: 20 Parables for Driving Home Your Point*
- *Doing Life With God: Real Stories Written by Students*
- *Doing Life With God 2: Real Stories Written by Students*
- *The Visual Edge: Compelling Video Connectors for Your Worship Experience*
- *Mission-Driven Worship: Helping Your Changing Church Celebrate God*
- *An Unstoppable Force: Daring to Become the Church God Had in Mind*
- *A Follower's Life: 12 Group Studies On What It Means to Walk With Jesus*
- *Leadership Essentials for Children's Ministry*
- *Keeping Your Head Above Water: Refreshing Insights for Church Leadership*
- *Seeing Beyond Church Walls: Action Plans for Touching Your Community*
- *unLearning Church: Just When You Thought You Had Leadership all Figured Out!*
- *Morph!: The Texture of Leadership for Tomorrow's Church*
- *The Quest for Christ: Discipling Today's Young Adults*
- *LeadingIdeas: To-the-Point Training for Christian Leaders*
- *Igniting Passion in Your Church: Becoming Intimate with Christ*
- *No More Lone Rangers: How to Build a Team-Centered Youth Ministry*

With more to follow!

THE QUEST for CHRIST

Discipling Today's Young Adults

KEN BAUGH
RICH HURST

Flagship church resources
from Group Publishing

Group's R.E.A.L. Guarantee to you:

This Group resource incorporates our R.E.A.L. approach to ministry—one that encourages long-term retention and life transformation. It's ministry that's:

Relational
Because learner-to-learner interaction enhances learning and builds Christian friendships.

Experiential
Because what learners experience through discussion and action sticks with them up to 9 times longer than what they simply hear or read.

Applicable
Because the aim of Christian education is to equip learners to be both hearers and doers of God's Word.

Learner-based
Because learners understand and retain more when the learning process takes into consideration how they learn best.

THE QUEST FOR CHRIST
Discipling Today's Young Adults
Copyright © 2003 Ken Baugh and Rich Hurst

Visit our Web site: www.grouppublishing.com

Credits
Creative Development Editor: Paul Woods
Chief Creative Officer: Joani Schultz
Editor: Beth Rowland
Copy Editor: Janis Sampson
Art Director: Jane Parenteau
Cover Art Director: Jeff A. Storm
Cover Designer: Blukazoo Studio
Print Production Artist: Jane Parenteau
Photographers: Daniel Treat and PhotoDisc
Production Manager: Peggy Naylor

Library of Congress Cataloging-in-Publication Data
Baugh, Ken.
The quest for Christ : discipling today's young adults / by Ken Baugh and Rich Hurst.
    p. cm.
Includes bibliographical references.
      ISBN 0-7644-2344-4 (pbk. : alk. paper)
        1. Church work with young adults. 2. Discipling (Christianity) I. Hurst, Rich. II. Title.
    BV4446.B385 2002
    259'.25--dc21   2002015628

10 9 8 7 6 5 4 3 2 1   12 11 10 09 08 07 06 05 04 03
Printed in the United States of America.

Contents

Dedication

To Jessy, Katy, Ari, and Jessa, and each generation to come.

Acknowledgments

It's true that no book happens in a vacuum; it takes a committed team. Without a caring God, Kim Hurst's editorial genius, and Susan Baugh's constant encouragement to dream and write, this book would have remained just a ramble of thoughts. We are indebted to them all!

Yet there are others on each of our teams as well—people who poured their lives into us through their godly example and commitment to helping each of us become godly men. Ken would like to thank his grandfather, Dr. Warren Herd; Dr. John Townsend; the Rev. Rick Warren; the Rev. Lon Solomon; and Dessia Crawmer. Rich would like to thank Bruce Larson, Frank Tillapaugh, Terry Hershey, and Trevor Bron. God has used each of these men and women to facilitate Christ formation in us. We're especially grateful to the Rev. Lon Solomon and the elders of McLean Bible Church, who have constantly encouraged us to be innovative in reaching new generations.

Finally, thank you to Paul Woods for believing in this project, Sue Geiman for believing in us, and Beth Rowland for her hard work.

Introduction

> " *Your system is perfectly designed to yield the result you are getting.* "
>
> —Business principle

> " *Therefore go and make disciples…* "
>
> —Matthew 28:19a

Loston Harris is an artist, an award-winning jazz pianist. He's played with some of the best jazzers of our day, most notably the great Wynton Marsalis. He's been praised by critics for the maturity of his sound, the deep understanding he brings to his interpretation of jazz standards, and the creativity of his own compositions and arrangements.

In 1999, while still in his twenties, Loston had hit a wall professionally and personally. He'd just finished several years on the road and a stint in Las Vegas. Having been raised in the church, with a dad in ministry, he'd been taught to live life a certain way and knew his life on the road had not matched up to his parent's expectations. With the kind of weariness that years living out of a suitcase can engender, he headed for home in northern Virginia unsure of his next move.

Loston sensed his life needed grounding and was even vaguely aware his life needed God; he just didn't know how to make the connection. He thought about visiting his parents' church, but he remembered how uncomfortable he'd felt there as a teenager. Like many in his generation, Loston felt the church didn't understand the things that were important to him. To Loston and his friends, art, music, and self-expression were highly valued. In his parents' church, these were either ignored or criticized. As he now thought about returning to his parents' church, he envisioned being scolded for his casual dress or facing the question of when he was going to settle down with a "real" job.

Driving around suburban Washington, D.C. one day, he vaguely remembered a church a friend had mentioned years ago. The friend had spoken enthusiastically about the crowds of young adults at this church, the warm atmosphere, and the sermons built around videotaped movie clips. Loston remembered wondering if his friend was talking about some kind of cult; the church he was describing sounded nothing like the church where he'd been raised.

Loston did some checking and learned the church service, called Frontline, was still meeting on Sunday nights at McLean Bible Church. He decided to check it out for himself.

"Immediately after arriving I knew this was something I was going to like," Loston recalls. "The people were so down-to-earth and welcoming. Immediately I sensed real community there. I loved it that people were just wearing casual clothes and hanging around together. Church for me in the past had been about dressing up and behaving very properly. Everyone wanted to check up on you and make sure you were doing the expected thing. Here, people didn't care what I did with my life, how important I was, or what I could do for them. They just wanted to be kind to me, regardless of who I was. In the music industry, there is so much pressure from people who want something from you. This was such a nice break from that."

> " Church for me in the past had been about dressing up and behaving very properly. Everyone wanted to check up on you and make sure you were doing the expected thing. Here, people didn't care what I did with my life, how important I was, or what I could do for them. They just wanted to be kind to me, regardless of who I was. "

Loston began attending Frontline regularly. He began to hear the gospel presented in ways that made sense to him as a young adult and as an artist. He began to want to study more on his own and really plumb the depths of the Bible. His dad saw what was happening and was grateful. After many futile years of trying to guide Loston toward a deep relationship with Jesus, his dad saw something had finally sparked Loston's imagination.

Loston was beginning for the first time to envision his own life in Christ. The relationships Loston had formed with other musicians and artists at Frontline, the weekly sermons based on contemporary themes, and the acceptance of Loston's individuality were all working together to create the right environment to incubate faith in Christ.

In October 2000 at his dad's side, Loston prayed and asked Christ to take over his life. Although he'd been raised in the church, God had used the ministry of Frontline to connect with Loston in a way that hadn't been possible until then. Loston continued to worship at Frontline and the other McLean services, using his musical gifts in the worship services and content to think that God might want him to spend his days playing music in church. But God had other plans, and after a year or so Loston moved to New York where he headlines nightly at the Carlisle Hotel, a jazz musician's dream come true.

> " The Great Commission tells us to 'go and make disciples.' It doesn't tell us to invite people to come to us; it tells us to go. It doesn't tell us to make converts; it tells us to make disciples. Unfortunately when it comes to this generation, that's no easy task. "

While our churches should be full of young adults like Loston, it is the unfortunate fact that churches are devoid of them because the Lostons out there don't come to church. Church doesn't make sense to many young adults; it doesn't address things that are important to them.

So what? Why should we care? Why can't young adults just get with the program and fit into our way of doing things? Why do we have to cater to their whims?

The answer is obvious of course. The Great Commission tells us to "go and make disciples." It doesn't tell us to invite people to come to us; it tells us to go. It doesn't tell us to make converts; it tells us to make disciples. Unfortunately when it comes to this generation, that's no easy task. You'll see in this book that today's young adults don't respond to the traditional methods of disciple making. Tried and true programs seem to have no impact on the hearts and minds of young adults like Loston.

BETTER SYSTEMS, BETTER RESULTS

As the opening quote reminds us, the results we're getting (fewer sold-out disciples of Christ in this generation) are due to the inadequate systems we've designed.

We believe that you'll see better results when you create better systems for discipling young adults. We have learned that developing young-adult disciples in this postmodern age requires a radical shift from the way we have historically ministered to and discipled people. In this book we'll explain how culture changes necessitate changes in discipleship and we'll describe what a new-generation friendly church looks like.

This book is based on six assumptions about discipleship:

1. Many discipleship programs are built on old models of content-based discipleship that will fail to transform a person in today's world.

2. Churches don't need discipleship programs that teach transformation as much they need to create environments where transformation naturally occurs.

3. Postmodern discipleship is not about doing disciple-making within a certain generation as much as it is about disciple-making within a certain mindset.

4. Many, but not all, young adults see the world from a postmodern perspective. This generation is heterogeneous, not homogeneous.

5. You cannot begin an effective discipleship ministry by creating programs and handing them over to young adults. They must create their own ministries and feel ownership.

6. Disciple-making among postmoderns does not mean abandoning or altering the message of the gospel.

A WORD ABOUT TERMS USED IN THIS BOOK

The terms we use in this book will be familiar to you. The context in which we use them may not be. To avoid confusion let's quickly discuss our use of these familiar terms.

Disciple: When we use the word disciple, we're referring to someone who has decided to become a follower of Jesus Christ not just a "Christian." A disciple is an individual who has committed to being a life-long student of the Master; someone learning to master life through imitating the Lord. We are not referring to the casual believer in Jesus; we are talking about someone who is intentional in his or her lifestyle and faith journey.

"Aren't all Christians disciples by default?" you might ask. No, they are not. See page 195 for a look at several Scriptures that bear this out.

Many writers have grappled with what constitutes an effective disciple and what makes for an effective ministry. It would be safe to say that faithfulness to the Lord, living a fruitful life of service, and having a passion for one's calling in life have historically been three general characteristics of a disciple.

> ❝ A disciple is an individual who has committed to being a lifelong student of the Master; someone learning to master life through imitating the Lord. We are not referring to the casual believer in Jesus; we are talking about someone who is intentional in his or her lifestyle and faith journey. ❞

Discipleship: We use the term discipleship in two ways. One way is the process every Christian undertakes to become more like Christ. Our own discipleship is the process of our being transformed by the renewing of our minds in Christ Jesus (Romans 12:2). Throughout this book we frequently use the term *Christ formation* to describe this process. Secondly, we use the term discipleship to describe the systems, methods, and environments we create to guide another along his or her journey of Christ formation.

Postmodernism: When we use the term postmodernism, we refer to a recent cultural shift which has made an impact in the arts, philosophy, technology, and the rest of society. The easiest way to understand postmodernism is to put it in the context of modernism, the cultural movement that precedes it.

A timetable is helpful here.

Prior to the modern period, during the Middle Ages, God was the center of life. Everything was looked at from a perspective that God was the creator and author of all life.

Gutenberg's invention of the printing press in about 1450 marks the end of the Middle Ages and the beginning of the modern age. The modern age is characterized by the assumption that it is man, not God, who discovers and creates. Man becomes the author of life. For the next five hundred years, philosophers, scientists, and explorers all provide substance to the argument that humans are central and God is peripheral.

Finally, in the late twentieth century, there began to be a shift in thinking. Globalization, brought on by the invention of the Internet, worldwide airplane travel, and multinational corporations, to name just a few factors, has ushered in the period of postmodernism.

> " To the postmodern mind, however, knowledge is important only in so far as it can be applied to an end. Knowledge must be useful, and it is acquired through experience. Emotion, imagination, and story are all valid means by which the postmodern person seeks knowledge. "

The differences between the modern age and postmodernism are clearly shown in the realm of knowledge acquisition, a subject that bears heavily on any discussion of discipleship. In modern societies knowledge is equated with science, and is contrasted with story. Science produces reliable knowledge, while story is considered unreliable and therefore not a source for knowledge. To the modernist, knowledge has its own intrinsic merit. One gains knowledge through education, experimentation, and exploration in order to be knowledgeable in general and to add to the world's catalog of things known.

To the postmodern mind, however, knowledge is important only in so far as it can be applied to an end. Knowledge must be useful, and it is acquired through experience. Emotion, imagination, and story are all valid means by which the postmodern person seeks knowledge.

The difference in how postmoderns acquire knowledge is just one example of the seismic shift in thinking that is characteristic of many young adults and the church leaders who hope to train them as disciples of Christ. Since the church in America is primarily an institution steeped in modernism, most church leaders have little idea how to connect with young adults in America.

In this book we'll look at the ways that postmodernism has affected today's young adults, especially in the area of spiritual development. We'll help the reader understand the essential components of true discipleship, the elements of any effective discipleship system, and we'll introduce the reader to a number of programs that have worked effectively with today's young adults.

ABOUT THIS BOOK

This book is divided into three parts:

Part One: **Preparations** includes a chapter that sets up our metaphor for discipleship and a chapter that introduces a new paradigm for discipleship.

Part Two: **Signs Along the Way** includes eight chapters that discuss the signposts our travelers in the quest for Christ will pass along the way. As long as they arrive at each signpost, the travelers will know they're on track in their quest.

Part Three: **Travel Tips** provides many ideas for how to put into practice the things you'll learn in the preceding chapters.

ABOUT THE AUTHORS

It might help to know a little about us as you begin.

Ken is an Xer (born in the sixties); Rich is not (born in the fifties). Ken is from a broken home; Rich is not. Ken became a Christian as an adult; Rich became a Christian as a child. Rich's involvement in young-adult discipleship has lasted more than twenty-five years; Ken's is more recent. We went to very different seminaries and yet our paths crossed, and we discovered we had the same passion to reach, train, and equip young adults.

Together we have come to understand the impact of postmodernism on this generation. Our journey together and the things we've learned about effective discipleship with this generation form the basis of this book. We hope you find lots here to encourage and enlighten you as you guide young adults in their quest for Christ.

13

HOW TO USE THIS BOOK

As you use this book, remember that it's about transformation, not information. The following steps will help you do this.

Step 1: Gather a group of interested people.

Step 2: Read through this book together.

Step 3: Answer the questions and do the exercises that are shown in the margins of each chapter.

Step 4: Divide and do these steps again with another group of people. For example, if there are two of you in the first group, then start two new groups; if there are four of you, start four new groups.

Here's a question to get you started thinking about discipleship and Christ formation:

• How would you summarize the goals and the hope of your Christian life?

PART ONE

PREPARATIONS

THE QUE8†

" *Your life is a journey you*
must travel with a deep
consciousness of God. "

—1 Peter 1:17

For years European students have taken advantage of what's called a "gap year" to travel and see a bit of the world. The gap year, a year-long interruption of one's formal studies, takes place sometime after high school and before or during the college years. For the most part, parents understand this pull on their children and recognize that low-budget travel, often by train and with a backpack, is a great way to get to know a place and one's self quite intimately.

More and more North Americans have begun to participate in the gap year tradition. Armed with not much more than a backpack, a train pass, and a Lonely Planet guide, young North Americans travel their way across Europe, making friends and learning lessons along the way.

For a moment imagine being such a student. You've decided you want to take a year to explore Europe, with no particular route in mind. You have a friend who made a trip like this a couple of years ago, and he's willing to go along with you. You're not sure where you'll go, but you know you'd like to visit several countries in Europe, covering the Scandinavian north, the Mediterranean south, the mountainous east, and the remote west.

Off you set on your quest to discover and explore Europe. Your friend proves to be a great help. Having been in Europe once before, he's got insights that help you get the most from your travels. Nevertheless, the two of you are discovering many new things together, for while your companion has made a similar trip once before, Europe is such a vast place that he's learning nearly as much as you are.

With no particular route in mind, you choose your next destination based on whim, available trains, or the suggestion of those you meet along the way. Outside each new train station and along each country road and motorway, you rely on signposts to keep you oriented to your present location and guide you toward your next destination. Because each signpost has arrows pointing in many different directions, you feel free to change direction when the mood strikes, knowing that as long as you eventually visit each of Europe's distinct regions you will have gained a familiarity with Europe. With each successive trip you make, you'll discover new insights and gain a more intimate understanding of the European continent.

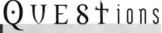

QUEStions

- What's the greatest journey you've ever been on?

- What parallels can you draw between that and your quest for Christ?

The quest for Christ, as we see it, is like this journey through Europe. Those who commit to becoming disciples of Christ are like these student travelers in three respects:

1. The goal of the journey is deeper understanding and intimacy with the subject, in this case, Christ.
2. Both the novice journeyer and the more experienced guide have much to learn. There is no point at which you finish gaining insights along the way.
3. The order in which you cover the terrain is irrelevant. No one area will give more insights than any other. What is important is that you explore all the different "regions" or elements of faith in Christ.

In this book we'll explore the various elements of discipleship. We'll be addressing you, to use the metaphor above, as the guide. In the next chapter we'll explore the final destination of the quest. In the quest to be a disciple of Christ, the ultimate destination is to be a person who loves God completely and loves others with the love of God. Part two of this book includes several chapters that will discuss signposts that will guide you along the way. When the journey is complete and you've taken your friend (or small group or congregation) past each signpost, you'll know you've done a good job of giving your friend a full picture of Christian discipleship.

QUEStions

- In what ways is Christ formation a journey?
- What is your definition of discipleship?
- How would you define the role of discipler?

A MAP OF CHRIST FORMATION

Before you can begin to explore Europe, you must first prepare for the trip. The first preparation is to know where Europe is and which countries or regions comprise it. The same is true with discipleship. Before you can guide someone on a journey toward Christ formation, you must understand the elements that define it. Only after you have grasped these elements and taken hold of their significance will you understand the territory you'll explore with another journeyer.

QUEStions

In your own words, define Christ formation.

Element 1:   Christ formation begins with God not man.

God calls us into relationship with him. The disciples did not choose Jesus, Jesus chose them. He approached them and called each one to follow him. This was Jesus' unique approach to discipleship that was different than other first-century master-disciple relationships.

This shows us the amazing grace of God—that he initiated a relationship with us. Romans 8:29-30 tells us that "God knew what he was doing from the very beginning. He decided from the outset to shape the lives of those who love him along the same lines as the life of his Son. The Son stands first in the line of humanity he restored. We see the original and intended shape of our lives there in him. After God made that decision of what his children should be like, he followed it up by calling people by

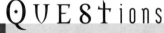

QUEStions

- How does God reveal himself to you?

- In what ways do you hope God will reveal himself to the postmodern young adults in your church?

name. After he called them by name, he set them on a solid basis with himself. And then, after getting them established, he stayed with them to the end, gloriously completing what he had begun" *(The Message)*.

Christ formation begins with God because it was he who first reached out to us in offering us the forgiveness of our sins and then inviting us into the lifelong process of becoming more like him.

Element 2:   Christ formation means knowing Christ personally and intimately, not just knowing facts about him.

Discipleship shouldn't be limited to mastering a body of biblical information. Knowing, memorizing, and studying the Bible are not ends themselves; they should point us to Jesus.

> " Discipleship shouldn't be limited to mastering a body of biblical information. Knowing, memorizing, and studying the Bible are not ends themselves; they should point us to Jesus. "

"When knowing facts about God, Jesus Christ, and the Bible takes precedence over a living relationship with Christ, the Sun goes into eclipse. When knowledge about Christianity becomes more important than entrusting one's life to Christ and being changed from the inside out, the church is in eclipse."[1]

The goal of discipleship is not to win a game of Bible trivia; we're supposed to come to know Jesus. Jesus was the *logos zoa*—the living Word.

John wrote, "The Word became flesh and made his dwelling among us" (John 1:14a). D.A. Carson says: "The Word, God's very Self-expression, who was both with God and who was God, became flesh: he donned our humanity, save only our sin. God chose to make himself known, finally and ultimately, in a real, historical man."[2]

God came to earth as man—the man Jesus Christ—partly to help us understand who God really is and what a life as a Christian (a little Christ) really looks like. As the writer of Hebrews says, "We don't have a priest who is out of touch with our reality. He's been through weakness and testing, experienced it all—all but the sin. So let's walk right up to him and get what he is so ready to give. Take the mercy, accept the help" (Hebrews 4:15-16, *The Message*).

> ❝ God was so concerned that we know him intimately and personally that he took on human flesh and moved into our reality! ❞

QUE8Tions

- What are the qualities you'd like to have in your life as a disciple?

- What would you like to characterize the lives of the young adults you disciple?

God was so concerned that we know him intimately and personally that he took on human flesh and moved into our reality!

Element 3: Christ formation means understanding our value because we are created in the image and likeness of God.

The value of a person has nothing to do with his or her performance; people have value because "God created man in his own image" (Genesis 1:27) and because Jesus died for them! Therefore God determines a person's value, and when we truly believe this, it changes the way we treat people.

Consider this story from Frontline. Matt was a young adult who started the homeless ministry in the early days of Frontline. At that time this ministry was our primary means of penetrating the inner city of Washington, D.C. with the gospel. Matt was doing a great job in leading this ministry, but due to a variety of factors he burned out and came to me (Ken) one day to resign. At that point I had a decision to make. As a pastor, I can walk a fine line between motivation and guilt.

I could have said, "Matt, common bro, suck it up. If you love Jesus, you'll keep going." I could have even quoted him a Bible verse to add a little biblical leverage: "Let us not become weary in doing good, for at the proper time we will reap a harvest if we do not give up" (Galatians 6:9).

I've done that before—shamed someone into compliance with my wishes. This time I decided to take a different approach.

I said, "Matt, you've done a great service for the Lord. Thank you!" And I left it at that. Matt felt valued and appreciated and went on his way.

About eight months later, Matt came to me and said, "Hey, Ken, I'm recharged and have a new idea. I met this guy named Tom, and he has an organization called Adopt-a-Turkey Foundation that matches a church's contribution dollar for dollar and feeds homeless and needy families turkey dinners at Thanksgiving. Do you think we could do this?" I said sure. So Matt went to work with renewed passion.

That year with Adopt-a-Turkey's matching funds, we were able to feed about two thousand needy people turkey dinners. That was five years ago. In 2001 through Matt's leadership, our church family fed 65,000 people turkey dinners on Thanksgiving.

I shudder to think that I could have blown this amazing outreach by not valuing Matt as a creation of God. I could have very easily "guilted" Matt into sucking it up with the homeless ministry, which he would have done for a time. But it wouldn't have taken long before he would have felt that he was being used and would have very likely walked away. We can use people to fulfill our own agendas or value them as created in the image of God. The former usually results in them becoming disillusioned and dropping out; the latter unleashes them to do the work of God. It was a great lesson for me to learn.

> " We can use people to fulfill our own agendas or value them as created in the image of God. The former usually results in them becoming disillusioned and dropping out; the latter unleashes them to do the work of God. "

Element 4: Christ formation teaches us that God is for us, not against us.

It's our opinion that most people believe in the god of their own opinions and subjective experiences instead of the God of the Bible. For example, if people believe that God loves them and is searching for them as a lover looking for his beloved, they respond positively. However, if people believe that God is angry because they did something wrong, they will hide and run away.

This was Adam's problem. He defined God based on his subjective belief. When Adam and Eve disobeyed God by eating of the tree of the knowledge of good and evil, their sin distorted their belief of God. They were afraid of him and hid. Yet, God went looking for them.

"But the Lord God called to the man, 'Where are you?' He answered, 'I heard you in the garden, and I was afraid because I was naked; so I hid.' And he said, 'Who told you that you were naked?' " (Genesis 3:9-11a).

In other words, God said, "Adam, where did you get a crazy idea like that?" Yes, God was angry at their sin. God hates sin, but he loves the sinner.

There's this crazy notion in people's minds that God is angry, that he is just waiting for them to make mistakes so he can throw lightning bolts at them.

Yes, God disciplines his children, but not as a result of anger or vengeance. God's dis-

QUEStions

- Do you see the notion that God is angry in the young adults you know?

- How can you help young adults get a more accurate picture of God?

cipline is motivated by love, and its purpose is training. In their book *How People Grow,* Henry Cloud and John Townsend say: "One of the biggest obstacles to growth is our view of God. If we are going to grow in relation to God, then we must know who God is and what he is really like...People do not grow until they shift from a natural human view of God to a real, biblical view of God...*People must discover that God is* for *them and not* against *them.*"[3]

Instead of believing that God is angry and waiting to punish us, we believe that God is for us and loves us; rather than running away from him and hiding, we run to him and confess. I've seen this played out with my daughter's poodle, Roxy.

When I let Roxy outside and she takes longer than I want her to (the winters are cold in Virginia), sometimes I get a little impatient and speak to her harshly, "Hurry up, Roxy, stop messing around." As a result of my harshness, she just cowers and hides. But if I talk to her gently, she does her business and comes obediently inside, wagging her tail and looking for her cookie.

> " Instead of believing that God is angry and waiting to punish us, we believe that God is for us and loves us; rather than running away from him and hiding, we run to him and confess. "

Our beliefs about God's response to our sin produce the same result. If we think God's angry, we will hide; but if we think God will respond with love—even if that love means discipline—we will move toward him. God is for us! Jesus paid the penalty for our sin. Jesus took the full wrath of God on himself. God has no wrath left for his children, only loving discipline. Help people see that God is for them.

Element 5: Christ formation shows us the importance of our relationship with other Christians.

God created us with a hunger to connect—a longing to be known and accepted at the deep levels of the soul.

During creation the only thing that God said was not good was that man was alone. "The Lord God said, 'It is not good for the man to be alone. I will make a helper suitable for him (Genesis 2:18).' "

> " Relationship is not only necessary for men and women; it's part of the image of God that can be seen in the fact that God himself exists in the community of the Trinity. Therefore, relationship is at the very foundation of God's nature. "

In order for people to thrive, they need to be in relationship, not just with God but with others, too. Relationship is not only necessary for men and women; it's part of the image of God that can be seen in the fact that God himself exists in the community of the Trinity. Therefore, relationship is at the very foundation of God's nature.

Henry Cloud, in his book *Changes That Heal,* says, "Relationship, or bonding, then, is at the foundation of God's nature. Since we are created in his likeness, relationship is our most fundamental need, the very foundation of who we are. Without relationship, without attachment to God and others, we can't be our true selves. We can't be truly human."[4]

And Erwin McManus says in his book *An Unstoppable Force,* "Spiritual maturity cannot exit outside of healthy relationships. In the same way, vibrant, spiritual ministry is the result of dynamic interdependence on other believers in the service of humanity."[5]

Christ formation in others largely depends on our ability to create safe places for people to be open and honest about their sin without

QUEStions

- Relationship is particularly important to young adults. How can you encourage relationship as part of discipleship in your church?

fear of condemnation. Without these safe places, people will not confess their sin, and without confession there can be no forgiveness, and without forgiveness people live in the deadly grip of isolation where the lies, accusations, and condemnation of the enemy will wreak havoc with their souls.

James refers to this in 5:16 when he says: "Make this your common practice: Confess your sins to each other and pray for each other so that you can live together whole and healed" *(The Message).* God wired the human heart to look for safe havens of grace, knowing that only there will we find the strength to confess our sins.

Isn't God enough? Of course, God is sufficient. Of course, God is the one who meets all our needs (Philippians 4:19). However, our theology of God's sufficiency is all wrong if it leads to a practice of rugged individualism or the idea that all I need is God and no human relationships.

God works through the living elements of his body. Don't ask me why, but that's what he does. In my opinion God could have chosen a much more effective means of transmitting his message of grace and love. Yet God has chosen to limit himself by using people as his messengers as Paul and Peter suggest:

"And he has committed to us the message of reconciliation. We are therefore Christ's ambassadors, as though God were making his appeal through us" (2 Corinthians 5:19b-20).

> However, our theology of God's sufficiency is all wrong if it leads to a practice of rugged individualism or the idea that all I need is God and no human relationships.

"Be generous with the different things God gave you, passing them around so all get in on it: if words, let it be God's words; if help, let it be God's hearty help. That way, God's bright presence will be evident in everything through Jesus, and he'll get all the credit as the One mighty in everything" (1 Peter 4:10-11, *The Message*).

Therefore the Church is the body of Christ, a living vine, where we are the branches and together constitute a spiritual community.

Element 6:   Christ formation means understanding godly sorrow.

There's a myth in many Christian circles that the primary means of behavioral change is to shame people into obedience. Make people feel bad enough about their sin, and they will change. The reality is that guilt results in condemnation and does not facilitate change.

This is what Paul is driving at in 2 Corinthians 7:10: "Godly sorrow brings repentance that leads to salvation and leaves no regret, but worldly sorrow brings death."

Guilt is worldly sorrow. Guilt causes us to try and atone for our own sin, which cannot work and results in death, which is separation from God. Godly sorrow, on the other hand, leads one toward change. Godly sorrow is a shift in our thinking: When we sin, we actually hurt God. "I have been hurt by their adulterous hearts which turned away from Me" (Ezekiel 6:9, New American Standard Bible).

When I believe that my sin actually hurts God—hurts the one I love and the one who loves me the most—I'm sorrowful and want to stop my sinful acts. This is what Paul refers to as "godly sorrow" and it "brings repentance." The distinction between "worldly sorrow" and "godly sorrow" is illustrated in the way Judas and Peter each dealt with their sin. Both Judas and Peter betrayed Jesus, yet they dealt with their sin in completely different ways. Let's take a look at Judas first.

"When Judas, who had betrayed him, saw that Jesus was condemned, he was *seized with remorse* and returned the thirty silver coins to the chief priests and the elders. 'I have sinned,' he said, 'for I have betrayed innocent blood.' 'What is that to us?' they replied. 'That's your responsibility.' So Judas *threw the money into the temple and left. Then he went away and hanged himself"* (Matthew 27:3-5, italics added). Judas admitted his sin, yet he tried to atone for it through his own efforts by hanging himself. Peter responded to the same sin much differently.

> Now Peter was sitting out in the courtyard, and a servant girl came to him. "You also were with Jesus of Galilee," she said. But he denied it before them all. "I don't know what you're talking about," he said. Then he went out to the gateway, where another girl saw him and said to the people there, "This fellow was with Jesus of Nazareth." He denied it again, with an oath: "I don't know the man!" After a little while, those standing there went up to Peter and said, "Surely you are one of them, for your accent gives you away." Then he began to call down curses on himself and he swore to them, "I don't know the man!" Immediately a rooster crowed. Then Peter remembered the word Jesus had spoken: "Before the rooster crows, you will disown me three times." And he went outside and *wept bitterly"* (Matthew 26:69-75, italics added).

Now what's important to notice is the two different ways that Judas and Peter dealt with their sin. Judas felt bad, he knew what he did was wrong, he even gave the money back, but none of that released him from the guilt and condemnation he was feeling. Judas dealt with his sin the world's way, and the world's way is always independent of God. Judas tried to even the scales, but it didn't work. Judas' way didn't get rid of the guilt, and it resulted in death.

Peter, on the other hand, dealt with his sin differently. He wept bitterly. He was broken because of his sin. The Bible doesn't say that Judas wept, only that he felt remorse. Weeping reveals an inner brokenness and repentance. It's not just feeling bad.

God responds to our brokenness over our sin, not just the fact that we are sorry we got caught. Psalm 51:17 says: "The sacrifice you want is a broken spirit. A broken and repentant heart, O God, you will not despise" (New Living Translation).

It's imperative in moving people toward confession of sin to understand the critical difference between worldly sorrow and godly sorrow. One leads to death; the other leads to confession, restoration, and life. Guilt is not good, and guilt is certainly not a tool God uses to motivate us toward obedience.

" We need to look at what the Bible has to say about the process and purpose of Christ formation because it appears that most current discipleship programs are not producing true disciples among young postmoderns. "

These six elements are the essentials of Christ formation. Unfortunately in many churches, these essential elements have been buried under layers of clutter. They've been turned into systems and programs that hide their true importance in the Christ-formation process. We need to strip away the clutter and take a fresh look at the core of disciple making. We need to look at what the Bible has to say about the process and purpose of Christ formation because it appears that most current discipleship programs are not producing true disciples among young postmoderns. Edwin McManus suggests we go back to zero: "For us to go back to zero means we must reengage the Scriptures, while at the same time detach ourselves from all of our assumptions in relation to methodology."[6]

QUESTIONS

- Why do you feel churches struggle to produce true discipleship among postmodern young adults?

CLEARING THE CLUTTER

Taking McManus' suggestion, let's look at the current assumptions that need to be cleared away before we can be effective disciplers.

Assumption 1: Discipleship is just another program in the church.

Discipleship should be a relationship between two travelers on their quest for Christ in which they spend time together in prayer, Bible study, and mutual encouragement. Instead, much of the discipleship programming that goes on in the church has been reduced to a twelve-week fill-in-the-blank teaching environment where the teacher shares with a student the essential

" It takes a lifetime for discipleship to be most effective, especially with postmodern young adults. The biblical truth being taught needs to be modeled in the context of real life. "

doctrines of the faith. It's not that this is bad—new Christians need to understand doctrine and theology, but this needs to be done in the context of a close relationship as a fellow traveler.

Christ formation cannot be reduced to this type of church program because discipleship takes longer than twelve weeks. It takes a lifetime for discipleship to be

QUE8tions

- What inaccurate assumptions about discipleship have you encountered?

most effective, especially with postmodern young adults. The biblical truth being taught needs to be modeled in the context of real life. Why? Because more is "caught than taught." Paul understood this principle. He told the Corinthians to "Follow my example, as I follow the example of Christ" (1 Corinthians 11:1). Instead of discipleship being reduced to a twelve-week formal program, the process of Christ formation should be viewed as the entire scope of a Christian's spiritual journey. Discipleship is holistic in that it defines the entire purpose of the Christian's life— to become like Jesus Christ. The role of

" The role of the Church in the discipleship process has more to do with creating the right kind of environment than figuring out the most effective programs. "

the Church in the discipleship process has more to do with creating the right kind of environment than figuring out the most effective programs.

Assumption 2: The goal of discipleship is behavior modification.

It's true that sinful behavior needs to be changed into behavior that glorifies and honors Christ. Yet, behavior modification is not the ultimate goal of discipleship. Instead, the ultimate goal of discipleship is transformation from the inside out. It begins with the heart and slowly moves into a person's behavior.

John Ortberg puts it like this: "When morphing [transformation] happens, I don't just *do* the things Jesus would have done; I find myself *wanting* to do them. They appeal to me. They make sense. I don't just go around trying to do right things; I *become* the right sort of person."[7]

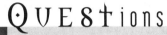

QUEStions

- What's the difference between information and transformation?

- Why is this difference important in the quest for Christ?

Jesus doesn't want just our outward obedience. He also wants the right motivations that lead to the right behavior. Obedience is a much deeper issue than behavior modification. Isaiah said: "These people come near to me with their mouth and honor me with their lips, but their hearts are far from me. Their worship of me is made up only of rules taught by men" (Isaiah 29:13).

In other words, their obedience was just "smoke and mirrors." This was Jesus' point as he confronted the Pharisees in Matthew 23:25-26: "Woe to you, teachers of the law and Pharisees, you hypocrites! You clean the outside of the cup and dish, but inside they are full of greed and self-indulgence. Blind Pharisee! First clean the inside of the cup and dish, and then the outside also will be clean." These religious leaders looked righteous on the outside. Their behavior was fine, but their hearts were twisted and corrupt.

When the goal of discipleship is to facilitate the inner transformation of a Christian, the behavior will eventually take care of itself. Dallas Willard makes this observation: "It is the inner life of the soul that we must aim to transform, and then behavior will naturally and easily follow. But not the reverse."[8] We need to be reminded that God is more interested in our hearts—when he has our hearts, he has our obedience.

Assumption 3: The current methods of discipleship are sacred.

Theology and methodology are not equals. Theology is how we understand God. Methodology is how we construct environments in which our theology is lived out in practice.

Methodology is not sacred and therefore can and must change and adapt to new methods that make sense in emerging cultures. Every generation has different characteristics, traits, and worldviews. "God uses different approaches to reach different groups of people. I'm not talking about churches deviating from biblical truth. The

> " Theology and methodology are not equals. Theology is how we understand God. Methodology is how we construct environments in which our theology is lived out in practice. "

message of Christ must never change."[9] Don't confuse methods with the message. The message must never change, but the methods must change with each new generation.

"The church must acclimate to a changing world, or she will destine herself to irrelevance or even extinction...For the first-century church, difficult and challenging environments caused her to thrive. The first-century church

QUEStions

- What discipleship methods are you familiar with?

- Which ones do you feel work best?

erupted out of a context of persecution. The church is designed to thrive on the edge of change and in the center of history. The church was designed to thrive in our radically changing environments."[10]

Why do we need

QUEStions

- What have you observed about young adult culture that sets it apart?

- Which discipleship methods do you think would resonate with postmodern young adults?

new methods with new generations? Because we reach different people groups in different ways. We've practiced this concept in cross-cultural missions for years. When Hudson Taylor went into China, he was the first western missionary to dress as the Chinese. He adapted to their culture without changing the Word of God. We need to view today's generations as a people group and apply the same philosophy of contextualization as Hudson Taylor did.

Assumption 4: We grow in spiritual maturity simply by studying the Bible.

Content-based discipleship is the name we give to the assumption that a person will grow in Christ simply by reading, studying, and memorizing Scripture. The truth is that Bible study alone does not lead to spiritual maturity. Jesus pointed this out to the Pharisees: "You have your heads in your Bibles constantly because you think you'll find eternal life there. But you miss the forest for the trees. These Scriptures are all about *me*!" (John 5:39, *The Message*).

Frankly, the true test of spiritual maturity isn't how much Bible I have under my belt. The true test of spiritual maturity is discovered by answering a sobering question: "Is my increasing knowledge of the Bible lending itself to a greater capacity to love people sacrificially?" This is what Paul was referring to in Philippians 1:9: "And this is my prayer: that your love may abound more and more in knowledge and depth of insight."

> " The true test of spiritual maturity is discovered by answering a sobering question: 'Is my increasing knowledge of the Bible lending itself to a greater capacity to love people sacrificially?' "

When a person reads, studies, and memorizes Scripture, he or she will quickly discover that the nature of God is love and that one who imitates God will live a life characterized by love. "Be imitators of God, therefore, as dearly loved children and live a life of love, just as Christ loved us and gave himself up for us as a fragrant offering and sacrifice to God" (Ephesians 5:1-2). Bible study is necessary for the renewing of our minds (Romans 12:2), for changing our worldview from secular to sacred, and for pointing us to the life and lifestyle of Jesus himself.

Having understood that Christ formation is defined by the six elements we've noted and having become aware of the layers of clutter that hide the true essence of discipleship with the four assumptions, you are now ready to begin the journey of Christ formation with young postmoderns. Together with another individual, a small group, or an entire congregation, you'll participate with others in their quest for Christ. Think of these six elements as the boundaries that encase the Christ-formation process, and the four wrong assumptions as roadblocks that might divert you from following a true course. Within the boundaries, signposts along the way will guide you through the quest for Christ, helping you reach the destination, which we define as living a life of love as a disciple of Christ. Let's talk more about the disciple's call to live a life of love.

NOTES

1. Leonard Sweet, *Aqua Church* (Loveland, CO: Group Publishing, Inc., 1999), 59.
2. D.A. Carson, *The Gospel According to John* (Grand Rapids, MI: William B. Eerdmans Publishing, 1991), 127.
3. Henry Cloud and John Townsend, *How People Grow* (Grand Rapids, MI: Zondervan Publishing House, 2001), 66.
4. Henry Cloud, *Changes That Heal* (Grand Rapids, MI: Zondervan Publishing House, 1992), 49.
5. Erwin Raphael McManus, *An Unstoppable Force* (Loveland, CO: Group Publishing, Inc., 2001), 172.
6. McManus, *An UnStoppable Force,* 187.
7. John Ortberg, *The Life You've Always Wanted* (Grand Rapids, MI: Zondervan, 1997), 23.
8. Dallas Willard, *The Divine Conspiracy* (San Francisco: HarperCollins, 1998), 144.
9. Rick Warren, *The Purpose-Driven Church* (Grand Rapids, MI, Zondervan Publishing House, 1995) 61.
10. McManus, *An UnStoppable Force,* 17.

The Destination
A LiFE OF LOVE

*" Be imitators of God, therefore,
as dearly loved children and
live a life of love."*

—Ephesians 5:1

In Matthew 22 an expert in the Mosaic law asked Jesus a question. "Teacher, which is the greatest commandment in the Law?"

We've come to know Jesus' reply as the Great Commandment: " 'Love the Lord your God with all your heart and with all your soul and with all your mind.' This is the first and greatest commandment. And the second is like it: 'Love your neighbor as yourself.' All the Law and the Prophets hang on these two commandments' " (Matthew 22:36-40).

QUESt

EXPERIENCE

- Watch the most recent version of the movie Les Miserables and describe the elements of sacrificial love you see in action.

In these few verses, Jesus is giving us the *CliffsNotes* on the entire Bible: Love God first and then demonstrate your love for God by living a life of love toward others. That's it! If you want to reduce the entire Bible to one theme, it would be love. If you want to reduce the goal of discipleship to a single goal, it would be love.

" If you want to reduce the entire Bible to one theme, it would be love. If you want to reduce the goal of discipleship to a single goal, it would be love. "

We would like to suggest that the church adopt a new paradigm for discipleship: love. Love is the calling, passion, and purpose of a disciple. And in the quest for Christ, our goal or destination should be living a life of love. Our lives should be characterized by a profound love for God and

QUE8†ions

- How has God's love affected your life?

- Why is love so important to our lives as disciples of Christ?

- How can you help young adults experience and practice God's love?

an active love for people. Christ said, "By this all men will know that you are my disciples, if you love one another" (John 13:35). Juan Carlos Ortiz says, "Love is not one of the elements of the Christian faith—it is *the* element. Love is the life itself."[1]

To understand what we mean, picture a cross. At the ends of each of the lines which form the cross are arrows. One arrow points up, one down, and one to each side. When you think of your role as a discipler, imagine guiding your friend in four directions, each represented by an arrow on the cross. The arrow at the top points to God, the one at the bottom to self. The arrows on either side point to fellow Christians on one side and non-Christians on the other.

Let's look at how the love paradigm of discipleship plays out in these four relationships.

RELATIONSHIP 1:
LOVING GOD THROUGH A LIFE OF WORSHIP

Jesus said that the first commandment is to "Love the Lord your God with all your heart and with all your soul and with all your mind" (Matthew 22:37-38). Mark adds *strength* (Mark 12:30). Jesus is telling us that loving God entails loving him with our entire beings: We're to put "no other gods" before him (Exodus 20:3). We're to give him our entire lives.

William Barclay says, "It means that to God we must give a total love, a love which dominates our emotions, a love which directs our thoughts, and a love which is the dynamic of our actions. All religion starts with the love which is total commitment of life to God."[2] This loving of God wholly manifests itself through a lifestyle of worship.

A lifestyle of worship simply means that every activity and thought of a disciple glorifies God. Paul says in Romans 12:1, "Therefore, I urge you, brothers, in view of God's mercy, to offer your bodies as living sacrifices, holy and pleasing to God—this is your spiritual act of worship." And in 1 Corinthians

> *" Jesus is telling us that loving God entails loving him with our entire beings: We're to put "no other gods" before him. We're to give him our entire lives. "*

10:31 he says, "So whether you eat or drink or whatever you do, do it all for the glory of God." Therefore, a disciple lives a lifestyle of worship by practicing the following daily habits:

QUEST

EXPERIENCE

Write a paragraph about the one thing (other than God) that you love most.

- How do you express your love toward that thing or person?

- Do you love God with the same passion and intensity?

- How do you express your love for God?

Habit 1: Living a life of gratitude

Calvin Miller says, "Praise grows from gratitude. Grateful for all that God has done for us, we feel a subtle stirring in the center of our hearts. Our thanksgiving erupts from those inner feelings of gratitude to God and his Son."[3] When a disciple reflects upon all that God has done to secure his or her salvation to provide the means of abundant life on earth through his indwelling Spirit, as well as the work that Jesus has been doing over the last two thousand years in preparing his or her home in heaven, the natural response is gratitude.

This lifestyle of worship reveals a thankful heart that is so full it spills out in praise to God and service of others. John says, "If anyone says 'I love God,' but keeps on hating his brother, he is a liar; for if he doesn't love his brother who is right there in front of him, how can he love God whom he has never seen? And God himself has said that one must love not

" " A person living a life of worship obeys the Lord's commands not out of fear and compulsion, but out of love and sincere appreciation. " "

only God but his brother too" (1 John 4:20-21, *The Living Bible*).

This life of gratitude comes from an inner attitude of the heart that says: "God, I'm so grateful to you for all you've done for me that I'll show you my appreciation by thanking you, being obedient to your commands, and loving others out of the abundance you have given me." A person living a life of worship obeys the Lord's commands not out of fear and compulsion, but out of love and sincere appreciation.

Q U E S t i o n s

- How can you encourage young adults to lead thankful lives?

Habit 2: Reflecting on the character and attributes of God

It's critical for a growing disciple to both understand and meditate on the character and attributes of God. He's the almighty God, faithful and righteous, who loves his children. A.W. Tozer notes the reasons this is so important. "Left to ourselves we tend immediately to reduce God to manageable terms. We want to get him where we can use him, or at least know where he is when we need him. We want a God we can in some measure control."[4]

Q U E S t i o n s

- How are God's attributes praised in your church?

- How does this practice affect discipleship?

We need to see God as he reveals himself to us, not through our own subjective interpretations or through the opinions of others. We must not create God in our own image. God created us to worship. If you don't believe it, just go to a rock concert or professional sporting event. People are worshipping. Of course, their worship is misguided, but nonetheless, these events illustrate our desire to worship.

We must worship God, because he alone is worthy of our worship. Dr. Wayne Grudem says, "But when God takes glory to himself, from whom is he robbing glory? Is there anyone who *deserves* glory more than he does? Certainly not! He is *worthy* of receiving glory."[5] In Revelation 4:11 the twenty-four elders surround the throne of God continually singing: "You are worthy, our Lord and God, to receive glory and honor and power, for you created all things, and by your will they were created." The seraphs in Isaiah 6:3 call, "Holy, holy, holy is the Lord Almighty; the whole earth is full of his glory."

When we worship God, we discover our true purpose and experience joy. Isaiah 43:7 tells us that God created us for his glory and Ephesians 1:12 notes that we were created

> " When we worship God, we discover our true purpose and experience joy. "

"for the praise of his glory." God created us for his glory and one of the ways we fulfill our purpose is to praise him for who he is. Further, as we praise him, we experience abundant joy.

Habit 3: Confession

Knowing the grace of God and his willingness to forgive leads us to confession; confession leads to God's forgiveness and our restoration to a right relationship with him. Henri Nouwen says, "Only in the context of grace can we face our sin; only in the place of healing do we dare to show our wounds; only with a single-minded attention to Christ can we give up our clinging fears and face our own true nature."[6]

QUE8tions

- How is confession an act of worship?
- How does confession affect a disciple of Christ?

That can be tough for some people. John grew up under the tyranny of an angry father. He was afraid to make even the slightest mistake for fear that his father would lash out at him with a barrage of verbal or physical abuse. The edict of the house was absolute compliance to his father's rules, or else. When John became a Christian, it was difficult for him to grasp the truth that God was his heavenly Father because of the abuse he experienced from his earthly father. So when John stumbled and sinned, he became deeply afraid that he would lose the love and favor of God. John needed two things: First, he needed to understand God's role as his heavenly Father; second, he needed counseling to work through his childhood abuse.

> " Unconditional love is simply a kind of love that looks out for the best interests of the other person; the kind of love that has no strings attached; the kind of love that can never fade, spoil, or perish. "

It's important for a new disciple like John to understand God's attitude toward people when they sin. The key point for them to understand is that when they sin, God is not angry but hurt. This is important because it reveals the type of relationship they have with God: a healthy father/child relationship that is based on unconditional love. Unconditional love is simply a kind of love that looks out for the best interests of the other person; the kind of love that has no strings attached; the kind of love that can never fade, spoil, or perish.

Habit 4: Obedience

Obedience is an expression of worship in that when I obey the commands of Jesus, I'm expressing my love and appreciation to him for what he's done for me. God isn't interested in compliance, but rather a heartfelt desire to live a life that is pleasing and honoring to him. Jesus said, "If you love me, you will obey what I command" (John 14:15).

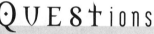

QUEStions

Describe the kind of obedience disciples are to practice.

• Do you see that evidenced in the young adults you disciple?

Obedience that is worship is obedience motivated by love for God and a desire to please him. This is the only type of obedience that God desires. Isaiah 29:13 says, "These people come near to me with their mouth and honor me with their lips, but their hearts are far from me. Their worship of me is made up only of rules taught by men." God doesn't want us to obey his commands because we have to, but because we want to.

Habit 5: Corporate worship

Corporate worship is when believers come together as the body of Christ and praise God through music, talk to God together in prayer, partake of the sacraments of remembrance, and open the Scriptures together in study. Corporate worship plays a major part in the process of Christ formation.

Too often we hear young adults downplay the role of corporate worship in their lives. They argue that going to the beach or mountains, playing golf, or simply taking a Sunday afternoon drive in the country is an adequate context to worship and praise to God. Perhaps this mindset is part of the developmental process of young adults as they get out on their own. With their newfound independence they're free to make decisions, and some for the first time have the ability to decide whether or not they even want to go to church. Yet, church attendance is much more than just a religious duty, it's a vital part of a growing disciple's life.

Brennan Manning agrees: "What is the relationship between discipleship and religious practices? The

QUE8tions

- How can you use your church's worship services to be a part of discipleship?

latter sustains the Christian life. It is impossible to keep Christian values in focus if we do not read Scripture and pray and lean on others for support and direction…We need reminders, symbols, stories, exhortations, living models, times out for reflection and celebration."[7] We believe that the context that best supports these elements that Brennan Manning is talking about can best be found in regular church attendance.

Habit 6: Private worship

While corporate worship is essential in the growth of a disciple, private worship plays a vital role as well. The essence of private worship is meditation and prayer. Meditation on the Word of God is a means of transport in which we experience the Scriptures through our imagination. Richard Foster says, "In this simple way we begin to enter the story and make it our own…Using the imagination also brings the emotions into the equation, so that we come to God with both mind and heart."[8]

This practice, referred to as *lectio divina* (divine reading), allows us to embrace the truths of Scripture—not just with our minds, but with all our senses. Ignatius of Loyola exhorts us to use all our senses in divine reading. "We smell the sea. We hear the lap of water along the shore. We see the crowd. We feel the sun on our heads and the hunger pangs in our stomachs. We taste the salt in the air. We touch the hem of his garment."[9] Through meditating on the Scriptures and using our imaginations, we create a powerful mechanism to experience God.

> " Meditation on the Word of God is a means of transport in which we experience the Scriptures through our imagination. "

QUEStions

- How can you encourage young adults to worship privately?

Prayer is the other element in private worship. Entire volumes have been written on prayer so we won't try to cover it in depth here. However, we feel the need to mention prayer because it's an essential part of the Christ formation process. "Prayer is the central avenue God uses to transform us…In prayer, real prayer, we begin to think God's thoughts after Him: to desire the things He desires, to love the things He loves, to will the things He wills."[10]

RELATIONSHIP 2:
LOVING MYSELF THROUGH SPIRITUAL DISCIPLINES

What did Jesus mean when he said, "Love your neighbor as you love yourself"? First, we must determine what it looks like to love oneself. Jesus' statement would seem to imply that in loving one's neighbor, one would look out for the other's best interests—to be a good neighbor would mean to do what's best for the other. If we apply this understanding to ourselves, it might look like this: "Love yourself as you love your neighbor." In other words, "Do what's best for yourself."

As you disciple young adults, you need to help them learn how to love themselves by doing what's best for themselves. In light of our discussion on the process of Christ formation this raises an interesting question: "What's best for myself as a disciple?" Surely this does not imply some type of hedonistic or narcissistic action. It has nothing to do with bolstering my self-esteem or

> ❝ As you disciple young adults, you need to help them learn how to love themselves by doing what's best for themselves. ❞

writing nice notes to myself to leave around the house. Instead, what's "best" for myself as a disciple are the practices that I must do to work out my salvation (Philippians 2:12-13).

To love myself as a disciple is to take an active role in my own growth. How do I do this? The answer lies in the very word *disciple,* a cognate of the word *discipline.* Thus, we can love ourselves as disciples by practicing spiritual disciplines.

Quite a bit has been written on the subject of spiritual disciplines.

QUEStions

- Do you practice the disciplines?
- Do the young adults you disciple practice the disciplines?

Brainstorm ways you could encourage the young adults in your church to practice spiritual disciplines.

Some have mistakenly thought that these disciplines help us gain favor with God—a means of earning extra credit or Brownie points. This of course is false. God's love for people is unmerited. His love is motivated solely by his mercy not our actions.

So what do these disciplines achieve? John Frye says, "Spiritual disciplines are powerful resources that allow us to encounter God in powerful—and sometimes unusual ways….[they are] simply a human activity that creates a space or setting for God to work."[11] Spiritual disciplines slow us down long enough for God to guide, comfort, and admonish us through the Holy Spirit.

Richard Foster's classic book *Celebration of Discipline* is one of many excellent resources that outline these disciplines. He discusses the "inward disciplines" of meditation, prayer, fasting, and study; the "outward disciplines" of simplicity, solitude, submission, and service; and the "corporate disciplines" of confession, worship, guidance, and celebration. While the practice of each discipline is important in creating space for God in the life of a disciple, we want to focus our attention on two specific disciplines that present great difficulty for many young adults: silence and solitude.

> " Spiritual disciplines slow us down long enough for God to guide, comfort, and admonish us through the Holy Spirit. "

In our first book, *Getting Real,* we noted in great detail the various forces that have shaped today's young adults. However one of those forces, perhaps one of the most devastating, is the divorce of parents that many young adults experienced when they were children. Many young adults whose parents divorced when they were young have painful feelings and memories of hurt, abandonment, rejection, and a suffocating fear of being alone.

While research has documented the effects of divorce on most young adults, my own (Ken) personal experience has shown its effects on me. My parents divorced when I was five years old. I have worked long and hard to come to the place in which I can see beyond the pain their divorce caused me. However, I still struggle with many of the same feelings of abandonment, rejection, low self-esteem, and the pervasive negative feelings in regards to being alone.

What, you ask, does this have to do with the disciplines of silence and solitude? Simply this: I will avoid anything that might trigger these feelings. The thought of being alone in a quiet place of solitude makes my skin crawl. I would much rather stay busy and look productive than subject myself to the potential pain of aloneness. Yet this place of solitude and silence is the very place that I need to be so God can transform me. Henri Nouwen says that "solitude is the furnace of transformation."[12]

It's in my times of solitude with God that he reveals to me those things in my life that need to change. Yet solitude is also important in that it deepens my relationships with others. Henri Nouwen goes on to say, "Without the solitude of heart, our relationships with others easily become needy and greedy, sticky and clinging, dependent and sentimental, exploitative and parasitic, because without the solitude of heart we cannot experience the others as different from ourselves but only as people who can be used for the fulfillment of our own, often hidden, needs."[13]

There is a profound tension here: The very thing I need for Christ formation and healthy relationships with others becomes the very thing I run from. If relationship with God and others is my greatest need, then those same relationships present my greatest fears.

In their book *Generation Alone,* authors William Mahedy and Janet Bernardi draw some disturbing conclusions. "[Aloneness] encompasses a basic distrust of people and a fear of being hurt. Aloneness is largely about fear. It stems from abandonment or neglect and leads to alienation from friends, family and society. Aloneness is a survival technique and comes across as independence. Aloneness separates this generation from every other."[14]

So how do I, as one who disciples young adults, help them work through these issues? I try to help them to remember that in silence and solitude they are not alone, that they are in the company of their heavenly Father who longs to scoop them up into his lap and love them, and that they're his beloved children whom he loves and longs to spend time with. And even though they might have a diminished capacity to experience and receive love due to many of the emotions of their parents' divorce, they'll find it comforting to know that God is there and that he loves them and understands their fears.

The personal challenge for those young adults who have experienced the pain of a family divorce is to not project onto God their feelings of rejection, abandonment, and aloneness. It will also help them to realize that even Jesus himself experienced some of these feelings. Hanging on the cross with the sin of the world on his shoulders, God turned from Jesus, and Jesus cried out in anguish, "My God, my God, why have you forsaken me?" (Matthew 27:46)

Jesus knows what abandonment feels like; he can empathize with our pain (Hebrews 4:15). Silence and solitude are two important disciplines of the Christ formation process. In order to help young adults of divorce to allow these disciplines into their lives, they need to understand ultimately that they're never alone.

RELATIONSHIP 3:
LOVING OTHER BELIEVERS IN COMMUNITY

It's imperative to help young adults understand their fundamental need for relationship with other believers. In the beginning, the only thing that God said was "not good" was that man was alone (Genesis 2:18). Why? The reason is simple. Every living organism is dependent on elements outside of itself to grow. A tree can't grow independently—it requires the sun, air, water, and rich soil to thrive. The same is true for people. Relationships are fundamental to the Christ-formation process. But why? Why can't a disciple grow alone?

Reason 1: Relationships with others provide comfort.

The bumper sticker that says, "Life is hard and then you die" smacks of truth. Jesus said, "In this world you will have trouble" (John 16:33). It's a given: Life is hard; trouble will come. And to make it through the hard seasons of life everyone needs the comfort of others.

Often God uses the pain and struggle we experience in life to help others going through the very same thing. Paul speaks to this in 2 Corinthians

 QUESTions

- What opportunities for community are available for young adults in your church?

- What can you do to encourage relationship and community?

1:3-4, "Praise be to the God and Father of our Lord Jesus Christ, the Father of compassion and the God of all comfort, who comforts us in all our troubles, so that we can comfort those in any trouble with the comfort we ourselves have received from God." We need relationships with others so that we can be comforted in times of difficulty.

Reason 2: People need others they can trust with their sinful parts.

An essential element to growth is facing our own sinfulness. If people can't face their own sinfulness, they can't repent and grow in Christlike character. To face our sinfulness, we need safe people.

Simply put, "Safe people are individuals who draw us closer to being the people God intended us to be…They are accepting, honest, and present, and they help us bear good fruit in our lives."[15] Safe people are individuals to whom we can bear our souls. A safe person is a trusted friend who can be told the truth no matter how vile and can be counted on to demonstrate unconditional love and acceptance. Everyone needs safe people to share their hurts, fears and dreams.

Larry Crabb says, "The power to meaningfully change lives depends not on advice, though counsel and rebuke play a part; not on insight, though self-awareness that disrupts complacency and points toward new understanding is important, but on connecting, on bringing two people into an experience of shared life."[16]

QUE8+ions

- Who has loved you unconditionally?
- How did they do it?
- How can you encourage unconditional love among young adults?

Paul reminds us that we need one another to grow. "Instead, speaking the truth in love, we will in all things grow up into him who is the Head, that is, Christ. From him the whole body, joined and held together by every supporting ligament, grows and builds itself up in love, as each part does its work" (Ephesians 4:15-16).

Reason 3: People cannot carry their own burdens all the time.

My wife Susan and I are involved in an intense fitness program. The goal of each weight-lifting session is to go until you simply don't have another ounce of strength left. I have to tell you, when I've got a sixty-five-pound dumbbell in each hand and am going for my final set, I'm sure glad Susan is there to spot me; she can give me a little of her strength to keep the dumbbells from falling on my face. Susan is a good spotter. She knows when I can make it on my own, and she knows when to step in and help.

"Spotting" is a spiritual principle and can be clearly seen in Galatians 6:2-5. In verse 2, Paul says, "Carry each other's burdens, and in this way you will fulfill the law of Christ." But in verse 5, he says, "Each one should carry his own load."

Paul isn't contradicting himself, but making an important point. At times things become so difficult that one cannot bear them alone. These are the "boulder" issues in life: a loved one dies, parents get divorced, a daughter is assaulted. Other believers must come along and help carry the burden. When we come alongside of others in this way, Paul says we are fulfilling the law of Christ, namely Jesus' new command to love one another (John 13:34).

At other times one must bear the responsibility for his own load. Paul refers here to those things in life that one should not expect another to do. I shouldn't expect handouts of food and money if I can work. These are my responsibilities and as such, I need to bear the burden.

Life can present issues of such magnitude that alone, any one of us would be crushed. We need others to spot us; we need others to come alongside us and supply a little bit of their strength to our load.

Reason 4: People can't heal alone.

Everyone has been affected by sin—the sins of others and the sins they have committed. These sins wreak havoc in our lives and cause intense pain.

> " A critical element to the Christ-formation process is healing deep in the heart of the disciple. God uses people to facilitate this healing process through love, understanding, and acceptance. "

This is where our need for people comes into play. James 5:16 says, "Therefore confess your sins to each other and pray for each other so that you may be healed." When a person confesses sin to another and experiences love and acceptance instead of shame and condemnation, healing begins to take place in his or her life.

A critical element to the Christ-formation process is healing deep in the heart of the disciple. God uses people to facilitate this healing process through love, understanding, and acceptance.

RELATIONSHIP 4:
LOVING UNBELIEVERS THROUGH COMPASSION

One night after a Frontline Communion service, I received an e-mail from a young adult named Janice.

Dear Ken,

Thank you for that amazing time of praise and worship last night. I'm glad that we aren't afraid to put the crucifixion of Jesus in its proper context. It had a major impact on some visitors, and I wanted to take a minute to share that with you.

I brought three guests with me last night. The first two were first-time visitors. The third person is a good friend of mine who has been to Frontline with me before. We have had many intense conversations regarding "religion" over the past six months.

After several months of attempting to "persuade" her through apologetic arguments and generally beating her over the head with the Bible, I realized that I needed to shut my mouth, walk the walk, pray, and let God take care of it. Well, last night was amazing. Her head was bowed during much of the service, and she appeared to be in prayer. Afterward she told me how moving it was and that she wanted to tell me a secret.

She never told me that secret, but she sent me an e-mail, which leads me to believe that she made a decision for Jesus. I wanted to share her e-mail with you. I have been amazed to see God work in her life over the past few months. He just kept breaking her and then drawing her close despite my many shortcomings. See her e-mail below:

Janice, thank you again for hanging out with us today at church. You were very kind and sweet to me and my friends and that is so great of you. After church today I was filled with an amazing feeling that I would like to keep to myself for now but wanted to let you know I had/have it. Thank you again. I had a great day!

QUEStions

Janice is obviously a believer who thought the most effective means of sharing Christ with her friends was by persuasive apologetics and using

- Does your church foster a sense of compassion toward non-Christians?

- What can you do to help young adults learn compassion?

her Bible as a weapon. Much to her surprise, it wasn't her persuasion that affected her unbelieving friend, but her compassion. A heart of compassion is what drives effective evangelism among today's young adults.

NOTES

1. Juan Carlos Ortiz, *Disciple* (Carol Stream, IL: Creation House, 1975), 43.
2. William Barclay, *The Gospel of Matthew, Vol. 2: The Daily Bible Study Series* (Philadelphia: The Westminster Press, 1975), 278.
3. Calvin Miller, *Into the Depths of God* (Minneapolis: Bethany House, 2000), 94.
4. A.W. Tozer, *The Knowledge of the Holy* (New York: Harper & Row, 1961), 13.
5. Wayne Grudem, *Systematic Theology: An Introduction to Biblical Doctrine* (Leicester, England: Inter-Varsity Press and Grand Rapids, MI: Zondervan Publishing House, 1994), 442.
6. Henri Nouwen, *The Way of the Heart* (New York: Ballantine Books, 1981), 17.
7. Brennan Manning, *The Signature of Jesus* (Old Tappan, NJ: Chosen Books, 1988), 67.
8. Richard J. Foster, *Prayer* (San Francisco: Harper San Francisco, 1992),147.
9. Ignatius of Loyola as quoted in Richard J. Foster, *Prayer,* 149.
10. Richard J. Foster, *Celebration of Discipline* (San Francisco: Harper San Francisco, 1988), 30.
11. John W. Frye, *Jesus the Pastor* (Grand Rapids, MI: Zondervan Publishing House, 2000), 102.
12. Henri Nouwen, *The Way of the Heart,* 13.
13. Henri Nouwen, *Reaching Out* (New York: Doubleday, 1975), 44.
14. William Mahedy and Janet Bernardi, *A Generation Alone* (Downers Grove, IL: InterVarsity Press, 1994), 21.
15. Henry Cloud and John Townsend, *Safe People* (Grand Rapids, MI: Zondervan Publishing House), 11.
16. Larry Crabb, *Connecting* (Nashville, TN: Word Publishing, 1997), 31.

PART TWO

SIGNS ALONG THE WAY

Signpost One _____

Imagination

> *" Imagination is more important than knowledge. "*
> —Albert Einstein

> *" All mortals tend to turn into the thing they are pretending to be. "*
> —C.S. Lewis, *The Screwtape Letters*

One of the signposts you'll pass on your quest with a fellow disciple is "Imagination." In this chapter we'll explore why imagination is so crucial to the Christ formation process. Let me (Rich) illustrate the importance of imagination with an example from my own life.

HOW IMAGINATION WORKS

In the course of our marriage, my wife Kim and I have bought three houses. Each of them had sat on the market for some time, passed over by other buyers who found them, let's say, less than charming. But budget restrictions are often the source of great powers of imagination. In the case of all three, we used our imaginations to see the homes these houses would become once we had the chance to put in some time and effort.

TRAVEL LOG

Here's an example of using imagination with young adults. When Frontline wanted John to take over the leadership of their short-term mission program, they asked him come and live with me for a week, to hang out and be discipled. Now in a modern context of leadership development, we would take someone through a leadership course or an orientation class, then give that person a job description. But instead, John and I spent the week doing building projects and talking about life and dreams and short-term missions. We wanted him to catch what needed to be done, not be told what to do.

The house we now own has a yard full of tall maples, mature flowering dogwoods, beautiful gardens, and a big stone fireplace in the large family room. Well, to be honest, it has none of that. Not yet anyway. But in my imagination it does. For now it has spindly little maple and dogwood saplings, piles of barren topsoil, and a sketch of the family room and fireplace we hope to add when we can afford to. Nevertheless, when I pull up in front of the house and look at the front yard, in my mind's eye I see everything the way I know it will look someday.

QUEStions

- What is imagination?

- Why did God create us with the ability to imagine? What purpose does imagination serve?

Anyone who plants a tree or puts in a garden is acting on imagination. The holes are dug and the plants watered and nurtured with full conviction of the end result. When I've planted a row of tulip bulbs, I don't stand back and admire the bare earth covering the bulbs. I stand back and imagine some future spring morning when I'll walk out the door to be greeted by a thick line of tall, proud tulip blossoms.

My journey with Christ is based on the same powers of imagination. The more I learn and grow in my intimacy with Christ, the more convinced I become of the need for even greater intimacy. I feed and nurture my relationship with God because I can envision a time when I'll be more like Christ, when I'll enjoy even deeper intimacy with my Creator.

QUEStions

- Why is imagination important in the quest for Christ?

In the same way, when I disciple a new believer, I imagine the time when he'll comprehend God's mercy, grace, and love with the certitude of a mature Christian. I nurture and tend his growing faith, as I would a young seedling, because I can envision his roots firmly planted in his own conviction of God's presence.

There's a difference, of course, between gardens and people. People make choices. They choose to obey or disobey, to follow or to go astray. While we can feel fairly certain of the outcome when we tend our gardens, we can't expect the same cause and effect with humans. This is why discipleship programs can be so vexing. Discipleship programs are usually predicated on the idea that if I can convince another to follow a set of behaviors (Bible study, prayer time, church attendance), he or she will someday live a sold-out life for Christ. Your own experience tells you this isn't true for many people, and it's certainly not true for postmoderns.

> " When I disciple a new believer, I imagine the time when he'll comprehend God's mercy, grace, and love with the certitude of a mature Christian. "

IMAGINATION AND THE POSTMODERN

Here's the thing you need to understand—and you probably do already—about postmodern thinking: Experience informs truth. This is to say no amount of teaching, cajoling, or reasoning will convince the postmodern mind of a truth until the postmodern spirit has experienced that truth.

> " ...no amount of teaching, cajoling, or reasoning will convince the postmodern mind of a truth until the postmodern spirit has experienced that truth. "

The statement, "Read your Bible and pray every day, and you'll gain a deeper relationship with Christ" is no motivator at all to the postmodern new believer who wants a more profound intimacy with God. How does she know your statement is true? The postmodern young adult is unlikely to accept your proposition as true just because you say it's true. She must be pulled along into acceptance of this truth by her own experience.

Hebrews 11:1 addresses imagination when speaking about faith: "Now faith is the substance of things hoped for, the evidence of things not seen" (New King James Version). Anyone with a sixth-grade science education understands that substance is something that can be touched, seen, or otherwise empirically known; yet through faith, we are told, we can experience things we only hope for. This is the aspect of imagination that's so important in Christ formation.

This is why imagination is so crucial in discipling postmodern young adults. As I said earlier, imagination allows us to suspend disbelief and fully accept something that has yet to be proven true.

QUEStions

- What is it you have faith in that you can't see? What role does imagination have in faith?

Imagination allows me to see fully grown maples where there are now only saplings. Imagination allows my daughter to be convinced she is a famous singer as she spends hours in her bedroom singing into a fake microphone. It allows me to imagine committing my entire life to God. It allows me to imagine igniting the holy imagination of an entire generation for Christ.

QUEStions

- Where do you want to be in your Christian life five years from today? How much do you think your imagination has to do with seeing that come to pass?

None of these things has happened yet, but the more I can imagine them and the more I experience them as true, the more I trust their eventuality and behave accordingly.

Amy e-mailed Ken after a communion service and said, "Ken, I'm not a Christian, but at Communion tonight I could feel God dripping off the walls. What do I need to do to start my journey with Christ?"

The goal in discipling postmoderns like Amy is to ignite in their own imaginations an experience that is compelling enough that it convinces them of truth. Remember, in biblical terms, truth is not a set of facts or concepts. Truth is a person, the person of God in Christ Jesus. Discipling, therefore, is providing the environment which helps others imagine their own intimate relationship with the Truth. When truth is a set of facts or a concept, the proper response is to say, "This is true. I believe." When Truth is a person, the proper response is to say, "Yes, you are true. I'll follow you anywhere. You have all of me."

We need to create environments where people meet the God of the Bible and that encounter ignites their imagination. We need to offer a milieu of ministry that moves people from being "unchanged believers," who have merely assented to the notion of God's love—"This is true. I believe." We long for a generation of changed believers—"You are Truth. I give you my all." The problem with the concept of discipleship as a program is that the

> ❝ Remember, in biblical terms, truth is not a set of facts or concepts. Truth is a person, the person of God in Christ Jesus. ❞

emphasis is placed on pursuing more knowledge about God. When discipleship is a program, the bottom line is activity, not intimacy.

Nevertheless, we understand your temptation to say, "Give me a plan, give me a program. Give me the how-to material!" It's an understandable temptation that makes it all the more imperative for us to clarify our intention before we go on. It's not our purpose to devise five easy steps that will guarantee discipleship

·QUE8†ions

- What would you like young adults to think about God? What can you do to spark their imagination?

success. It's not our purpose to design a program that will eliminate failure. Granted, it would be nice to have such a guarantee.

But we cannot get away from the fact that any success you experience from the implementation of ideas shared in this book must be based on an understanding of the importance of imagination in the process. We start from the point of view, in the words of German theologian Dietrich Bonhoeffer, that "Christianity without discipleship…is always Christianity without Christ."[1]

> ❝ Discipleship in many churches has meant bringing people to a place of compliance with expected behaviors. This approach doesn't fly with today's young adults. ❞

Discipling others is not getting them to do what you want. It's helping them develop a new way of thinking for themselves. As we walk with others in their journey toward intimacy with God, we assist them in developing their own Christocentric worldview, a point of view that sees everything with a mind transformed by Christ. Discipleship in many churches has meant bringing people to a place of compliance with expected behaviors. This approach doesn't fly with today's young adults.

IMAGINATION AND THE POWER OF STORY

We spark the postmodern young adult's imagination by helping him or her gain an accurate picture of God. Communicating the intrinsic nature of God takes place, for the young adult, through story. Jesus knew all about sharing stories and inviting others to journey. He called the twelve and spent time with them, telling them stories as they walked around the dusty roads of the Middle East. He spent three years with them, not ten weeks going through a curriculum. Then he sent them out to try out his stories of how they were to live.

QUESTions

- Think of something that happened in your quest for Christ that has shaped your understanding of God. How could you tell that story to young adults to spark their own imagination?

The greatest story we can talk about is our faith story. The problem comes when people hear us say, "Let me tell you about my faith." Too often they stop us out of fear that we're going to tell them about the God of the Western church. They're surprised when instead we tell them about our own journeys and invite them to come along. As we walk them through our own stories, they have a chance to see God at work in our lives and can begin to imagine their own lives transformed by Christ's love.

" Do you want to reach postmodern young adults? Then ask them to join you in your day-to-day activities. Better yet, join them in theirs. "

This method of sharing love through stories speaks to postmodern young adults and is a more effective discipleship tool than a whole library of self-guided Bible studies. Do you want to reach postmodern young adults? Then ask them to join you in your day-to-day activities. Better yet, join them in theirs. Run errands together. Meet for lunch during the workday. Send instant messages to their computers at work. Give them a ride when their car's in the shop. All the while, share your story. Ask about theirs. Show them the places in their own lives where God is present, offering love and grace.

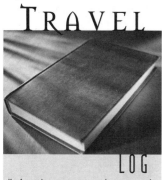

TRAVEL

LOG

You're only one person, and you can only make this kind of investment in a few lives. That's why community is so important. And there's more about the power of community in later chapters.

THE LOSS OF HIERARCHY

Many of today's young adults live in a world where they are evaluated by their effectiveness, not their intrinsic value as persons. This might come from the modern business world, in which there is tremendous emphasis on effectiveness: How does it work? Is this the fastest way? Did it get results?

For business leaders to achieve the results they seek, they often develop hierarchical chains of command within the company to maximize effectiveness. This emphasis on effectiveness has trickled into all aspects of society (such as the family, for example—remember the myth of "quality time"?).

Sadly, effectiveness has become the measure by which we judge our efforts at discipleship. Does this technique "work"? Is there a faster way? Will this method reach more people? As a result of this emphasis on effectiveness, the individual is often overlooked, at best, or made the target of a program, at worst. To a generation that highly values individuality and self-expression, this focus on effectiveness is a turn off.

Another by-product of this business-like approach to discipleship is the tendency toward

> " To a generation that highly values individuality and self-expression, this focus on effectiveness is a turn off. "

hierarchy, in which the person doing the discipling is the only one with any power. Instead of two friends sharing a journey, there's a leader and a follower, a boss and a subordinate.

It's important that we differentiate here between power and responsibility. Not all persons in a relationship have the same authority or the same area of authority. One may even be responsible to the other, and in that way, come under his or her authority. In the same way, one may be responsible in that several others report to him or her.

To assume, however, that this implies a difference in power (or the capacity for power) is a qualitative distinction. Power implies ownership and a capacity to effect change. If that property is limited to "the top," then we discourage imagination, and the best we can hope for is that someone will do exactly what we tell them. In discipleship that means the people we disciple would never learn to think and dream on their own.

In the imagination model, ideas are limitless. Every person has the ability to serve God as a co-equal image bearer, and therefore every person has the capacity to effect change. Each has the power to make decisions, to have choices, to give input, to solve problems, to plan the future, and to take responsibilities.

> " In the imagination model, ideas are limitless. Every person has the ability to serve God as a co-equal image bearer, and therefore every person has the capacity to effect change. "

Granted, it's a fantasy to think that power is (or can be) distributed equally to all participants. But that's not the alternative. This is not an all-or-nothing scenario we're painting in which there's the hope for utopia. The question we must ask is, does the system encourage the person? Are creativity and imagination encouraged and affirmed? Are people being empowered and transformed?

Let's pause for a moment to talk about those to whom we commit to disciple. If you are a pastor or large-group leader, you'll have a part in discipling anyone who walks through the door. But what about those who want to put together a small group or disciple another one-on-one? Again Jesus is our example here.

Can you imagine Jesus saying, "You know, Father, you asked me to find some disciples. But you haven't been to Galilee lately, have you? There aren't exactly discipleship-quality folks here. I mean, the best I could find is a fisherman who swears a lot, a tax man who steals from the people and the government, and two brothers who bring their mother everywhere!"

Jesus knew his job was not to wait for charismatic, exuberant, "together" people to appear for duty. He knew his job was to build disciples. His job was to spend time challenging people and igniting their imagination toward what they could do if they followed God. And the process began with selecting people who were, at the time, gems in the rough.

I suspect that there are many people in our churches (or organizations) who are, at best, gems in the rough. We may need to return to our place of ministry with new glasses. It means identifying those individuals who have a learning and giving heart. Skills can be taught, but people with a desire to grow and learn are a resource too precious to pass by.

Once we've identified the disciples we'll spend time with, the next step is teaching a lifestyle worldview. It's at this point that we

·QUE8†ions

- As a discipler, what could you gain through sharing imagination with a growing disciple? What could the disciple learn through sharing imagination with you?

·QUE8†ions

- Spend some time imagining what the young adults in your church could become. How does imagination affect your plans, your dreams, and your programs? How does imagination fuel your vision?

must make a choice in our style of ministry. It's a choice between program management and lifestyle modeling. We don't want to imply that these are mutually exclusive categories, but they are choices that determine values and priorities in our ministries.

Program management emphasizes efficiency. It's primarily task oriented. Lifestyle modeling emphasizes transformation. It's primarily people oriented.

Lifestyle modeling begins with a commitment to create a holistic environment. As a ministry leader, I need to commit to the resolution that my primary job description is to develop disciples. My primary task is not to accomplish certain goals, administrate certain projects, or execute certain programs. My primary job is to create an environment in which people can be transformed to accomplish their dreams and goals.

This goes back to the old saying that we must learn to be the people of God before we can do the work of God. In a purely program-management style, power is divided and held by those in charge. People are recruited to carry out the work efficiently. Business meetings are held to iron out problems that block efficiency. Don't get us wrong. A good deal of work does get accomplished using this scenario. But isn't there more to faith than im-plementing programs?

> " My primary task is not to accomplish certain goals, administrate certain projects, or execute certain programs. My primary job is to create an environment in which people can be transformed to accomplish their dreams and goals. "

Here's why I ask. Before I had made the shift in my own thinking, the primary reason for meeting with people was to accomplish tasks. There was no relationship other than the job. I think there were two reasons for that. One, when power is allocated and held by the few, those with power tend to mistrust the others. And two, it's easier to relate to someone if the connection is primarily task oriented. Real relationships—which include conflict, affirmation, stretching, risking, learning, and trusting—are never easy or efficient.

QUE8tions

- What methods could you use to spark your own imagination? Consider reading children's Bible story books and Christian allegory. Look at the world with "What if?" and "How about?"

The shift to lifestyle modeling affects one's calendar. It means that the primary purpose for gathering becomes mutual support, not checking in on the other's activities. It means that you attend fewer meetings, but you invest yourself more in each one. You may say no more often. And you'll find that you are no longer the only discipler in your ministry. The privilege of discipling is spread around among the members.

You can be sure that this style of ministry will get a reaction. It wasn't long in my own church before the grapevine was buzzing with the rumor that "Rich just isn't available anymore." At first it made me defensive.

Then I realized it was a myth to assume that I could be (or should be) available to meet everyone's needs. It was a myth that was built on the premise I had to do the discipleship or it didn't count.

In part, the rumors were right. I wasn't available to everyone. But I was very available to help create a holistic ministry of grace, truth, and journey.

> "Real relationships—which include conflict, affirmation, stretching, risking, learning, and trusting—are never easy or efficient."

In that environment, young adult disciples became partners in their own Christian growth and, rather than waiting for me to tell them their next step, they began to imagine for themselves what it would look like to follow Christ fully.

We've talked a lot about creating the right environment for imagination to flourish in this chapter. In the next chapter, we'll discuss the signpost of "Grace and Truth," and again we'll talk about creating the right kind of environment. It isn't our intention to tell you how to set up a weekly calendar of events that will provide an environment of imagination, hope, or any of the signposts we'll discuss in the next several chapters. We trust you'll come to understand why each of these signpost concepts is so important and will create your own environment (whether in a large church, a small group, or a one-on-one relationship) that reflects these concepts.

NOTES

1. Dietrich Bonhoeffer, *The Cost of Discipleship* (New York: Touchstone, 1959), 59.

Signpost Two _____
GRACE AND TRUTH

" To grow, we need things that we do not have and cannot provide, and we need to have a source of those things who looks favorably upon us and who does things for us for our own good. The Bible teaches that if we have faith in God, we are in an entire life situation of grace. "

—Henry Cloud and John Townsend, *How People Grow*

" We have seen his glory, the glory of the One and only, who came from the Father, full of grace and truth. "

—John 1:14b

H er name was Kate, and she walked up to me (Ken) one night after Frontline. Her face was strained, but in her eyes I saw a glimmer of hope.

Kate told me her story. She said, "I was on my way to kill myself tonight, but I thought I would give God one more chance. I had heard about Frontline from a friend who said that it was a great place where a bunch of young people gathered to study the Bible and hang out. And everyone is really nice, and you can sense the presence of God."

QUESTIONS

- When have you experienced God's grace?

- How did it affect your life?

I had taught that particular night about the grace and love of God. I had stressed the fact that God loves his kids no matter what and that he is more willing to forgive and restore us to himself than we are to admit and receive his love. Coming from a works-oriented church background, Kate hadn't grown up understanding the message of grace and rarely, if ever, had she felt the love and acceptance that she felt that night at Frontline. She started her life over that night.

> " Jesus came full of grace and truth and invites those who would follow him as disciples on a journey of life transformation, of Christ formation. "

Over time Kate began to grow in her faith and gained a new understanding of herself and God's love for her. Eventually she became one of the core leaders at Frontline and led some of the largest outreach projects. It was the love of God that Kate experienced that night through the Frontline community that convinced her that life was worth living in the light of the love of God.

As we've said, Jesus was all about love. John 1:14 tells us, "The Word became flesh and made his dwelling among us. We have seen his glory, the glory of the One and Only, who came from the Father, full of grace and truth."

QUEStions

- Are the young adults in your church fully experiencing God's grace? Why or why not?

Jesus came full of grace and truth and invites those who would follow him as disciples on a journey of life transformation, of Christ formation. But this transformation does not happen in a vacuum, nor is it the sole result of one-on-one time with God. Instead, transformation is forged within loving relationships composed of two primary ingredients, grace and truth.

THE JOURNEY: JESUS' CALL TO FOLLOW HIM

Jesus chose twelve men to follow him, to watch him live out grace and truth in the context of relationships. Jesus' goal for these men was to teach them to be "fishers of men." This leads us to a very important question:

How do you catch the hearts of men and women? Simply by grace and truth. There are a number of examples where Jesus modeled this for the disciples, but my favorite is the story of the woman caught in adultery.

> The teachers of the law and the Pharisees brought in a woman caught in adultery. They made her stand before the group and said to Jesus, "Teacher, this woman was caught in the act of adultery. In the Law Moses commanded us to stone such women. Now what do you say?" They were using this question as a trap, in order to have a basis for accusing him. But Jesus bent down and started to write on the ground with his finger. When they kept on questioning him, he straightened up and said to them, "If any one of you is without sin, let him be the first to throw a stone at her." Again he stooped down and wrote on the ground. At this, those who heard began to go away one at a time, the older ones first, until only Jesus was left, with the woman still standing there. Jesus straightened up and asked her, "Woman, where are they? Has no one condemned you?" "No one, sir," she said. "Then neither do I condemn you," Jesus declared. "Go now and leave your life of sin" (John 8:3-11).

The elements of grace and truth are found in verses 10-11. First he delivers grace: "Has no one condemned you? Then neither do I condemn you." Then he spoke truth to her: "Go now and leave your life of sin." He didn't just say: "It's OK, don't worry about it, everyone makes mistakes."

Leon Morris notes:

QUE8†ions

- Do young adults see you living out grace and truth?

- How can you model grace and truth?

"He tells her to sin no more. The form of the command implies a ceasing to commit an action already started: 'Stop your sinful habit'. And the 'no more' points to the thought of no return. She is to make a clean break with sin."[1]

I'm sure the disciples standing nearby were totally dumbfounded. A woman caught in the act of adultery, condemned to be stoned to death according to the Mosaic Law, is pardoned and given another chance by Jesus.

That second chance allows us the opportunity to grow and be changed from what we were before. However, while the goal of a believer's life is to become like Jesus Christ, that will not happen completely until we die and go to heaven. 1 John 3:2-3 says, "Dear friends, now we are children of God, and what we will be has not yet been made known. But we know that when he appears, we shall be like him, for we shall see him as he is."

There is, however, a fundamental expectation in the New Testament that we become conformed to the likeness of Christ while we yet live. "For those God foreknew he also predestined *to be conformed* to the likeness of his Son" (Romans 8:29, italics added).

QUEST

EXPERIENCE

Think of a time you were given a second chance. Describe how that opportunity affected you.

The Greek word for "to be conformed to" *(summorphous)* refers to both the internal and external transformation of a person.[2]

The word *summorphous* "indicates a likeness to Christ that is not just an external or superficial resemblance. It signifies the whole set of characteristics or qualities that makes something what it is…Our being made like Christ is not an arm's-length transaction. What we come to have, we have *together* with him."[3]

This is what Jesus was referring to in John 15:1-8.

> I am the true vine, and my Father is the gardener. He cuts off every branch in me that bears no fruit, while every branch that does bear fruit he prunes so that it will be even more fruitful. You are already clean because of the word I have spoken to you. Remain in me, and I will remain in you. No branch can bear fruit by itself; it must remain in the vine. Neither can you bear fruit unless you remain in me.

I am the vine; you are the branches. If a man remains in me and I in him, he will bear much fruit; apart from me you can do nothing. If anyone does not remain in me, he is like a branch that is thrown away and withers; such branches are picked up, thrown into the fire and burned. If you remain in me and my words remain in you, ask whatever you wish, and it will be given you. This is to my Father's glory, that you bear much fruit, showing yourselves to be my disciples.

When we stay connected to him, we bear the kind of fruit he bore: "But the fruit of the Spirit is love, joy, peace, patience, kindness, goodness, faithfulness, gentleness and self-control" (Galatians 5:22-23a).

It's interesting to note here that the supreme virtue for a disciple is love. The first fruit of the Spirit is love. 1 Corinthians 13:13 Paul said that love was the most important thing in: "And now these three remain: faith, hope and love. But the *greatest of these is love* (italics added)." Peter said, *"Above all, love* each other deeply" (1 Peter 4:8, italics added). Even Jesus said the entire Scriptures can be summed up in love.

THE ESSENCE OF GRACE AND TRUTH

God loves us and wants to transform us. As disciplers, we want to see God transform people too.

But church leaders often misunderstand how God goes about the business of changing people. Church leaders have got to get it into their heads that

QUEStions

- Evaluate how you go about discipleship. Do you focus on information or transformation?

- How might you assist young adults in being transformed by God's grace and truth?

spiritual growth is not merely the result of hearing the truths of Scripture—information does not equal transformation. Instead, God transforms lives through two essential forces: grace and truth.

Let me tell you how God used grace and truth to transform my life.

By the time I was twenty-one, I had pretty much messed up my life through a series of moral compromises. I had received Christ as my Savior at age twelve, but once I was on my own I started numbing my own pain through the abuse of alcohol and sex.

At age twenty-one I was tending bar and working in restaurants that placed me in environments rich with opportunities for moral compromise. The woman I was living with became pregnant and thought abortion was the only way out. I pressed her to get married, but she chose to have an abortion without my knowledge. The day she came home after the abortion, I hit rock bottom. I finally came to my senses and realized the gravity of my sin—I was now an accessory to the murder of an unborn child.

> " Church leaders have got to get it into their heads that spiritual growth is not merely the result of hearing the truths of Scripture—information does not equal transformation. "

Over the next few weeks our relationship slowly deteriorated, and I found myself alone with extreme guilt, shame, and intense feelings of condemnation. Sitting on the beach one day in southern California in my bankrupt spiritual state, God reaffirmed his love for me and his willingness to cleanse me of my sin. On that day, I recommitted my life to Christ and vowed to become a champion for grace and truth in my generation.

My story is one of a prodigal who has come home to the love of the Father. And I am deeply committed to both sharing my story as well as my encounter with grace and truth, which has shaped me into the man of God that I am today.

Someone might ask, "Do grace and truth really transform a person's life?" I can affirm that they do and, along with the Apostle Paul, I can say: "Here is a trustworthy saying that deserves full acceptance: Christ Jesus came into the world to save sinners—of whom I

QUEST

EXPERIENCE

Take some time to reflect. Consider those you know who have been transformed by God's grace and truth.

• How did it happen for each person?

Spend some time praising God for his love and transforming power.

am the worst. But for that very reason I was shown mercy so that in me, the worst of sinners, Christ Jesus might display his unlimited patience as an example for those who would believe on him and receive eternal life" (1 Timothy 1:15-16).

THE GRACE AND TRUTH OF GOD

Grace is simply unmerited favor. It derives its meaning from a Hebrew term that means to stoop or bend down. It's a picture of royalty walking by and reaching down to a peasant.

Grace is seen most clearly through acceptance and a willingness to help those who need help. Jesus never used the word *grace* in the gospel accounts, but he lived it out.

> " Grace is seen most clearly through acceptance and a willingness to help those who need help. Jesus never used the word grace in the gospel accounts, but he lived it out. "

He lived it out with a tax collector named Matthew and a man named Peter who betrayed him three times. He lived it out with a woman caught in adultery, a woman sitting by a well, and a prostitute who came and washed his feet with her tears. Jesus lived out grace with the lepers, the blind, the lame, and the demon possessed. Jesus modeled grace by

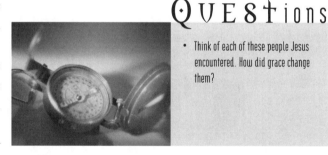

QUESTions

- Think of each of these people Jesus encountered. How did grace change them?

feeding the five thousand and by his compassion for the multitudes because they were like sheep without a shepherd. He lived out grace by raising a child from the dead and then giving her back to her mother; by raising Lazarus from the dead; and by healing the daughter of Jairus, the woman who had been bleeding for twelve years, and the centurion's servant. Jesus lived out grace with so many people, yet his ultimate expression of grace was demonstrated by his death on a cross to pay the penalty for our sin.

Not one of these examples merited the grace of Jesus. Not one deserved

> ❝ Not one of these examples merited the grace of Jesus. Not one deserved his stooping down. Yet through his unco ditional love and acceptance of each one, he was willing to help. That's grace! ❞

his stooping down. Yet through his unconditional love and acceptance of each one, he was willing to help. That's grace!

Truth, on the other hand, reveals our sinful human condition and points us to the solution. "There's nothing like the written Word of God for showing you the way to salvation through faith in Christ Jesus. Every part of Scripture is God-breathed and useful one way or another—showing us truth, exposing our rebellion, correcting our mistakes, training us to live God's way. Through the Word we are put together and shaped up for the tasks God has for us" (2 Timothy 3:16-17, *The Message*).

Q U E 8 † i o n s

- Is truth a part of your discipleship with young adults?

- What is the discipler's role with truth?

Q U E 8 † i o n s

- How has God revealed his truth to you?

- What was your response?

Truth tells us plainly that our hearts are twisted and sick with sin, that we love darkness instead of the light. Truth reveals our inner motivations and our total depravity and the fact that we cannot change ourselves. Truth reveals God's holiness, justice, and righteousness. Truth says that God cannot tolerate the smallest speck of sin, and all sin, no matter how small, must be paid for by death. Truth reveals how seriously God takes sin.

> ❝ Truth says that God cannot tolerate the smallest speck of sin, and all sin, no matter how small, must be paid for by death. Truth reveals how seriously God takes sin. ❞

Truth comes to us through God's Word—God's special revelation to us. The Bible is necessary to tell us and show us that sin needs to be confessed and behaviors need to change. The Bible gives us a mirror that helps us see what's wrong with our lives. But this truth by itself will lead to legalism. The law kills. That's what Paul was desperately trying to get the Galatians to understand.

> Oh, foolish Galatians! What magician has hypnotized you and cast an evil spell upon you? For you used to see the meaning of Jesus Christ's death as clearly as though I had waved a placard before you with a picture on it of Christ dying on the cross. Let me ask you this one question: Did you receive the Holy Spirit by trying to keep the Jewish laws? Of course not, for the Holy Spirit came upon you only after you heard about Christ and trusted him to save you. Then have you gone completely crazy? For if trying to obey the Jewish laws never gave you spiritual life in the first place, why do you think that trying to obey them now will make you stronger Christians? (Galatians 3:1-3, *The Living Bible*)

Henry Cloud and John Townsend address this danger in *How People Grow.*

> When we are under the law—in our natural state—we feel that God is the enemy and that we get what we deserve. We naturally try to "earn" life. We try to do whatever we think will get God to like us or whatever we think will solve our day-to-day problems. Thus, we are trying to "save ourselves" (see Matt. 16:25). We try to get God to not be mad, and we try by our own efforts to grow and resolve our issues. Yet Paul says that this way of living is the exact opposite of living according to faith and grace and that if we choose that law, we end up living out the law in real life. This is not just theology; it is exactly how people end up living their real-life problems until they grasp the reality of grace. And the result is failure.[4]

You see we need both truth and grace: We need the law to show us what's wrong, but we need grace to help us embrace the truth about ourselves.

" Truth and grace together teach us acceptance and forgiveness offered solely by love. They enable us to look at the condition of our hearts and cry out in anguish and repentance knowing that our heavenly Father is just waiting to run to us and forgive. "

Grace is the place of unconditional love and acceptance that is found in God and in "safe" relationships with other Christians who model for us the grace of Christ.

Truth and grace together teach us acceptance and forgiveness offered solely by love. They enable us to look at the condition of our hearts and cry out in anguish and repentance knowing that our heavenly Father is just waiting to run to us and forgive.

- What happens when there's too much emphasis on truth?
- What happens when there's too much emphasis on grace?
- Why is balance necessary?
- Do you keep grace and truth balanced in your discipleship efforts?

Jesus says to us, "I know the truth about you. You are sinful through and through. Yet if you are willing to face the truth about yourself and admit you can't change it on your own, I will offer my help. If you confess your sin to me, then I will forgive you and restore you into a right relationship with myself and others."

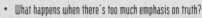

- How does an understanding of grace and truth affect your emotions and your thoughts about God?

Truth and grace are the two primary ingredients for growth. Truth shows us where we need to grow, and grace provides the accepting environment where we want to grow.

And this is good news for postmodern young adults. When they understand grace, they know that they can stop trying to earn God's favor because God's love for them is unconditional. Truth, on the other hand, provides the structure many of them long for but might not have received from their parents.

Far too many of today's young adults had parents who left them alone to navigate the turbulent waters of morality alone, where they were rarely told what was right and what was wrong. So now when they hear that Jesus is inviting them to follow him on a journey and watch how he lives out grace and truth with others, they experience grace and truth in a whole new way that leads them into a life of Christ formation.

QUEStions

• If you were to purposefully watch for evidences of God's grace and truth in the lives of young adults, what would you see? Try it!

NOTES

1. Leon Morris, *The Gospel According to John: The New International Commentary on the New Testament* (Grand Rapids, MI: William B. Eerdmans, 1971), 67.
2. William Edwy Vine, James A. Swanson, and John R. Kohlenberger III, *Vine's Expository Dictionary of New Testament Words* (Waco, TX: Word Books, 1998), 229.
3. Millard J. Erickson, *Christian Theology* (Grand Rapids, MI: Baker Books), 982.
4. Henry Cloud and John Townsend, *How People Grow* (Grand Rapids, MI: Zondervan Publishing House, 2001), 9.

Signpost Three ─────────

SOUL

" *The great malady of the twentieth century, implicated in all of our troubles and affecting us individually and socially, is 'loss of soul.'* "

—Thomas Moore

" *Come to Me...and you will find rest for your souls.* "

—Matthew 11:28-29, NKJV

The soul is very big these days. Soul sells. As a matter of fact, the publishing industry noticed a few years back that any book with the word *soul* in the title seemed to sell well: *Chicken Soup for the Soul; Soul Survivor; Soul Mountain; Leading With Soul.* People seem to be very much in touch with the part of them that is neither physical nor emotional, yet profoundly affects both: the spiritual part, the soul.

The coffee house phenomenon is a good example of this. And I'll admit, I (Rich) get sucked in like the rest. I love going to Starbucks coffee houses, and I don't even like coffee. Never touch the stuff. I go there because the place has soul. Starbucks is all about experience, and I want experience. Starbucks reinforces the idea that people are not commodities, but living souls. You can purchase cheaper coffee elsewhere, but you would have trouble finding better atmosphere.

Starbucks isn't the only place that understands the postmodern drive to feed the soul. Take a look at the corporations that market to young adults these days. Auto manufacturers say nothing about their cars' driving performance in their commercials; they talk about the sound systems, the space available for rolling out sleeping bags, the similarities between their cars and, say, your dorm room. The Gap runs ads with celebrity musicians saying nothing much in particular, with lighting and camera angles that make it difficult to see if the person is even wearing Gap clothing. But the ads convey a soulfulness that is lost on the concrete linear crowd and speak right to the heart of the postmodern.

People are spiritual beings. Everywhere you turn, people are pursuing spirituality through drugs, meditation, book clubs, and even through the kinds of foods they eat or the exercise programs they choose.

A few months ago we were having trouble with one of our horses. She was lame and generally out of sorts. The vet couldn't quite pin down the source of her trouble, so a racehorse trainer who lives nearby suggested we call in her friend, an equine masseuse. (Who knew?!)

Gwen, the masseuse, showed up and did her thing. As she massaged here and applied light pressure there, she asked what I did for a living. I told her I was a pastor, a comment

QUESt

EXPERIENCE

- With your group of fellow travelers, go to your favorite hangout and make a list of all the reasons you like that place.

- How would you describe that place to someone who wasn't with you?

- How could you create a similar atmosphere in your faith community?

- Why is atmosphere important to a postmodern young adult?

- What kind of atmosphere would you like to create within your church?

that often shuts a conversation down cold. Gwen seemed to feel she'd found a kindred spirit. She explained that she works with horses because "they are the most spiritual things there are." I asked her more about her love for her profession, and we chatted until the treatment was over and Gwen took her leave.

A month later I received a phone call from Gwen. "Does your church take donations?" she asked. She explained she was preparing to make an

QUEStions

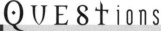

- How do various ethnic groups or groups with non-Christian spiritual beliefs create soulful environments?
- Why do they find soulful environments important?
- What benefits do they get from the environment they create?
- What principles can you apply to your church?

end-of-the-year contribution and wanted to send it to our church. "You're the most down-to-earth minister I've ever met," she said. Gwen, like nearly everyone else, is looking for soul.

Postmodern people are keenly aware that they have a soul. They believe strongly in the spiritual world. To their ears, we lag behind in our ministries with all our talk of "Six Ways to a Better Life" and "Teaching Your Teenager to Respect You." To the postmodern world, these talks sound far too simplistic. We need less emphasis on the science of ministry and more emphasis on the soul of ministry.

QUEStions

- How do different Christian groups (Pentecostals, Baptists, Episcopalians, Quakers) create soulful environments?

We have tried to understand why most churches cripple rather than enable true discipleship. We think the underlying issues, which discourage or encourage discipleship, are really

QUEStions

- In Acts 2 how did the disciples create a soulful environment?

- Which of those techniques can you apply to your situation?

pretty simple. But because they seem so normal, they have been deceptively difficult to grasp. Here are the five things we believe cripple the discipleship quest:

1. Concentrating on controlling people rather than empowering them.
2. Concentrating on training a few, not all, Christians.
3. Managing people rather than leading them.
4. Failing to communicate that God has created everyone for a special purpose of his choosing.
5. Using and reusing the same familiar methods rather than finding new ones.

CREATING A SOULFUL ENVIRONMENT

As we've said many times in this book, creating the right environment is essential for discipling young adults. Whatever your ministry context, whether you pastor a large group or work one-on-one with another disciple, there are certain factors to keep in mind as you work to create a soulful environment.

TRAVEL

LOG

We are suggesting you consider the mystery that appeals to so many when you plan your discipleship environment. Plan an environment that will allow for more chaos and less control. Be realistic as you plan for the time a discipleship model like this will take, keeping in mind that soulfulness cannot always be communicated in a tidy six-week program.

Factor 1: Disciple making is "job one."

Church building is too often confused with disciple making. Many times we build churches for the sake of having churches. But Jesus didn't commission us to build churches: he commissioned us to make disciples. Jesus never gave the church permission to be an end in itself. The church is to be the presence of the kingdom of God here on earth. When Jesus said, "Go and make disciples," he was bent on proclaiming and enlarging the kingdom of God.

Building a church for the sake of having a church has the same traps as building a business: Success becomes the driving force. We expect bottom-line profit motives to drive business, but Christian and non-Christian alike have an inkling that a church should be about something more profound.

Unfortunately, churches in America often grow in numbers without engaging people in a context relevant to the Great Commission, Matthew 28:18-20. "All authority in heaven and on earth has been given to me. Therefore go and make disciples of all nations, baptizing them in the name of the Father and of the Son and of the Holy Spirit, and teaching them to obey everything I have commanded you." Church growth principles can enable churches to grow using marketing techniques similar to the business world to appeal to those who are "church shopping." But successful numerical growth should only be part of the story.

Church growth does not guarantee discipleship. Church growth and church discipleship are not the same thing. And Jesus showed a clear prejudice toward discipleship.

The first words of Jesus' public ministry were "The time has come…The kingdom of God is near" (Mark 1:15). Throughout his entire ministry, Jesus relentlessly proclaimed the kingdom. In fact, he even told his followers to seek the Kingdom first.

> ❝ The church is the vehicle, the Kingdom is the objective, and what we are called to do for the Kingdom is make disciples. ❞

The most telling passages indicating the priority of the kingdom are found in Matthew 28 and in the opening and closing chapters of the book of Acts. The opening chapter in Acts sums up Jesus' post-resurrection ministry with his disciples by simply stating that he spent forty days speaking to them about the kingdom (Acts 1:3).

Acts 1 describes the prime time of Jesus' ministry. It answers the question "If Jesus had just one more opportunity to teach, how would he use it?" The fact is, he didn't zero in on church growth, rather he taught about the Kingdom. Later, at the conclusion of Acts, Paul is under house arrest in Rome where for two years "boldly…he preached the kingdom of God" (Acts 28:31).

QUESTions

- In Acts 1 what was Jesus telling people to do?
- In Acts 2–28 how did Jesus' followers follow his instructions?
- In Acts 28 what was Paul telling people to do?

Between Acts 1 and 28, New Testament Christians planted a lot of churches. Since the church is the primary vehicle of God's work on earth, it would be difficult to overstate its importance. And that is exactly the point. The church is the vehicle, the Kingdom is the objective, and what we are called to do for the Kingdom is make disciples.

That raises the questions, Just what is a disciple? and What is the kingdom? Perhaps Jesus gave the most succinct definition in the Lord's Prayer:

"Your kingdom come, your will be done on earth as it is in heaven." In short, God's kingdom breaks into human history whenever and wherever God's will is done. While Christians disagree over what form or portion of God's kingdom has or will come to earth, we all agree that we desire God's will to be done everywhere. God's kingdom translates into his will being done wherever an obedient disciple is.

QUE8†ions

- What does it mean to be "kingdom people"?

Those who are committed to discipleship think differently than those whose loyalties are to a particular church, denomination, or Christian organization. The challenge of disciple making extends beyond the normal church agenda to every facet of society. The idea of kingdom and the mandate for discipleship determine a church's value system and therefore dictate how a church invests its resources. Remember, our lives are shaped primarily by what we take for granted. And most Christians take for granted that the objective is to build churches in order to have churches. Therefore, they invest much of the church's resources into worship, while discipleship is given secondary support.

Church growth is not unique to our era, but the results are devastating. We have more mega-churches and fewer and fewer community churches, and all the while our church attendance is declining.

Factor 2: Disciple making is for everyone.

While a typical church stifles the church's discipleship, a soulful church enhances it. It levels and widens the playing field so everyone can be involved in the process of discipleship. At the moment, the laity play the church discipleship game on a field tilted against them. In a typical church we take for granted that its the ministers who do discipleship. But in a soulful church, people think differently about the ministers and discipleship. As a result, the discipleship game can be played on fields that are level and wide enough for everyone to play. In other words, discipleship is for the average person, not just the professional.

One of the central tenants of Luther's Reformation cry was the priesthood of all Christians. Laity, according to Luther, could read and interpret the Bible and confess their sin directly to God. The Reformation gave communication with God back to the laity, but it failed to give them permission to be ministers for God and to do what he commanded. We need a second Reformation that applies the priesthood of Christians not only to communicating with God but to doing what God wants as well.

While Protestants agree theologically that every Christian is a minister and that everyone is called to make disciples, we can't seem to practice it. The major obstacle is our view of the clergy. In our gut, we feel the reverend, the pastor, and the preacher really are closer to God than lay people. And it is really their job to

QUEStions

- What does it mean to be priests?

- How does soulfulness apply to the doctrine of the priesthood of Christians?

make disciples. We live as if we believe that God has laid claim to a few special people, and the rest are free to chase the corporate dream.

Imagine what would happen if we lived as if we believed that God calls every Christian to "go and make disciples." After all, the Bible teaches that the call of God upon one's life is not a prerogative given to a special few. Instead of the dramatic example of the Apostle Paul's calling on the road to Damascus, we do better to look again at his challenge to the entire church at Philippi: "Work out *your own* salvation with fear and trembling. *For it is God* who works in *you both to will and to do for his good pleasure*" (Philippians 2:12b-13, NKJV, italics added).

That is an incredible statement. We are told to work out whatever God is working in. Jesus' Great Commandment is a part of working out our salvation. Paul promises God will work in us to give us the desire and the ability to work out whatever he wants us to do. The most important mission challenge for the church is not to grow numerically. While healthy churches usually do grow numerically, that is not the ultimate goal. Rather the goal is to create a climate conducive for everyone to live out the Great Commandment.

In a typical church, the programs are designed from the top down. If the clergy really are in a special class that is closer to God, they should disciple everyone. In a soulful church, members understand their proper place in the priesthood and sense a freedom, even a drive, to make disciples.

Factor 3: Soulful disciple making requires ever-changing methods.

First Corinthians 9:19-23 says,

> Though I am free and belong to no man, I make myself a slave to everyone, to win as many as possible. To the Jews, I became like a Jew, to win the Jews. To those under the law I became like one under the law…so as to win those under the law. To those not having the law I became like one not having the law…so as to win those not having the law. To the weak I became weak, to win the weak. I have become all things to all men so that by all possible means I might save some. I do all this for the sake of the gospel, that I may share in its blessing.

This passage is great news for those of us who enjoy shaking things up a bit! Too many of us have been caged in by the sense that certain methods are inviolate. While the Christian message is absolute, the methods by which it is communicated are up in the air. The only methodological imperative is that our methods cannot distort the Christian message.

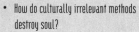

QUESTions

- How do culturally irrelevant methods destroy soul?
- How can our methods help to create a soulful environment?
- How will this help young adults grow in Christ?

Could it be that God intended discipleship of the church to be carried out through average Christians doing the things they naturally do? Could it be that it's OK to create discipleship approaches that tie into the culture we're targeting rather than asking the culture to meet us on our turf? Of course, it is! It's time to release ourselves from the obligation to make our ministry fit the methods devised in another era for another generation.

Devising strategies for Christians to do the things God asks them to do should not be that hard, but it is. Why? First, churches rarely attach any ministry value to discipleship. After all, our priority is to build a church. Second, we forget that average people have not been trained. Third, we institutionalize methodologies, which keeps us from creating the necessary new strategies.

> " Could it be that it's OK to create discipleship approaches that tie into the culture we're targeting rather than asking the culture to meet us on our turf? Of course, it is! It's time to release ourselves from the obligation to make our ministry fit the methods devised in another era for another generation. "

When desire and training come together to create new ministries, new methodologies are often necessary. Our church began a church within a church; it was a corporation within a corporation. The business world does it all the time.

Keeping methodology "up for grabs" in any organization is tough. But the church should have an advantage. After all, there is no methodological mandate in Scripture, just a Great Commission. The message is everything; the methods are incidental.

Factor 4: Soulful disciple makers are partners, not parents.

A soulful environment will produce disciple makers who understand the process of journeying alongside another, not out in front. In a soulful church, everyone is aware of a continual need for God's grace. Like Paul, we each see ourselves as "chief" among sinners. In this kind of environment, no one disciples another out of a sense of superiority.

Again, Philippians 2 is helpful here. This chapter is the Bible's most significant "incarnation" passage. Verses 4 and 5 sum up the challenge of chapter 2: "Let each of you look out not only for his own interests, but also for the interests of others. Let this mind be in you which was also in Christ Jesus."

The mandate for every Christian is the challenge to have the mind of Christ. And the mind of Christ demands that we be concerned not just about our own interests but also the interests of others.

Factor 5: Soulful disciple makers are gracious.

The other day I received a call from a not-so-recovering drug and sex addict named Tom, a young man I'd been discipling before he disappeared and stopped answering phone calls.

"Will you give me a second chance?" he asked, and I sensed the nervousness in his voice.

"Tom," I answered, "you're still on your first chance as far as I'm concerned. I didn't give up on you. I was just waiting until we were back in touch again. I'm glad you called."

We chatted some more about life in general, set an appointment, and hung up. There was no lecture on personal responsibility. I didn't scold Tom or tell him I'd only meet with him if I saw effort on his part. I just told him I was glad we were going to begin meeting again and discussing his faith.

QUE8tions

- How do we give people a second chance? Be specific.

- How will this affect them in terms of their sense of soul?

Like the merciful servant in the parable, disciple makers who have received great mercy feel compelled to show that same mercy to others. And this kindness, born of humble gratitude and lacking any pretense, is what attracts postmodern young adults. This skeptical generation is put off by those who act superior and drawn to those willing to acknowledge their need for mercy.

There will always be those who present a less-than-perfect picture of a disciple: the know-it-all; the one who's always late; the one who, like

> " This skeptical generation is put off by those who act superior and drawn to those willing to acknowledge their need for mercy. "

King David, commits some enormous lapse in judgment and obedience. Yet the soulful church contends that what we are—or rather *whose* we are—is more important than what we do. According to the Westminster Catechism, the highest calling for humankind is simply to glorify God and to enjoy him forever. According to Jesus, loving God with all our heart, soul, and mind is the first commandment. Disciple makers who understand this don't quit at the first sign of weakness, but stay committed to those bent on loving God.

Factor 6: Soulful disciple makers discourage overcommitment.

Many young adults will say they feel closer to God while hiking in the mountains, on a desert road, or on a path in the woods than they ever do at church. Maybe this is because churches can be so frenetic. A high-octane worship service one day, Bible class the next, volunteering at the food bank the third, singing with the worship team, attending a small group, helping with the youth group—our devotion to Christ is often measured by our willingness to overextend ourselves.

> ⁴⁴ Our devotion to Christ is often measured by our willingness to overextend ourselves. To a young adult, this is lunacy. The Apostle Paul said, 'But one thing I do,' and not 'These forty things I dabble in.' ʼʼ

To a young adult, this is lunacy.

The Apostle Paul said, "But one thing I do," and not "These forty things I dabble in." Disciple makers in a soulful environment will understand this and help each other avoid the trap of overcommitment.

QUE8†ions

- Pull out your calendar and show your fellow travelers how much time you have scheduled to spend with God.

- How does time with God affect your soul?

- Does scheduling time with God squelch your soul or refresh it? Explain.

I love the story of the explorer who hired local villagers to carry his gear as he made his way into the jungle. He was pleased after the first day when their progress was far better than he'd expected. Yet on the second day, the porters refused to move. Questioned about the stall, they

> ⁴⁴ Postmoderns see, often better than the rest of us, this disconnect between soul and body that characterizes modern society and even the modern church. They don't want to have any part of a system that not only allows that kind of disconnect, but rewards and encourages it. ʼʼ

explained that they had worked so hard and covered so much ground the first day, they now had to wait for their souls to catch up to their bodies.

Postmoderns see, often better than the rest of us, this disconnect between soul and body that characterizes modern society and even the modern church. They don't want to have any part of a system that not only allows that kind of disconnect, but rewards and encourages it. They are attracted to disciple makers who measure Christian maturity by full-

ness of heart, not fullness of calendar. When we journey with the postmodern young adult toward intimacy with Christ, we must be no less conscious of the intangibles of the

- Consider the intangibles of the soul—how does your church experience speak to those intangibles?

- What could you do to make your church's programs resonate deep within the soul of young adults?

soul than the marketers at Starbucks and other corporations have taught us to be.

Signpost Four ————————

R18K

" *When they saw Peter and John*
and realized that they were
unschooled, ordinary men, they were
astonished and they took note that
these men had been with Jesus. "

–Acts 4:13

My (Rich's) wife Kim was an Awana Club leader for several years. Though she complained bitterly about her uniform (think: extremely un-hip bowling shirt, gray with red trim), she liked the idea that our kids were becoming familiar with Scripture early in their lives, and she considered fashion suicide a small price to pay.

Awana, in case you haven't heard, is a Bible club program for kids where Bible memorization is highly valued and rewarded. The drill is that kids learn verses at home, come to club, spout them off, and get the pages in their books signed. Enough pages signed, and you get a reward (a pin, fake dollar to spend at the Awana store, a patch, or whatever).

As a kid moves through the book, he or she learns a sort of systematic theology of the plan of salvation, with verses building on each other until the astute kid has a pretty good idea of human depravity, our need for a Savior, and Christ's salvific act of redemption (well, in so many words).

As a dad, I was as thrilled as the next guy to see my kids begin to rack up a vest-full of patches. Even more important to me was that my kids grew in their knowledge and love of the Creator. But there was a problem Kim had to deal with. It wasn't the kids—they were eager to do well and learn the verses. The thing that frustrated Kim was the need of certain parents to prove their worth as loving parents by making the whole Awana experience a rat race for their kids. Too many parents were so intent upon having their kids succeed at the Awana *method* that their kids missed the *message.*

There were nights when Kim pulled parents aside and gently suggested, "Your daughter is really going through the book quickly. She seems to have a wonderful memory and a sharp mind. But there are times when we ask her to repeat verses from a few weeks ago or to tell us in her own words what they mean, and she seems stumped. Perhaps it might be a good idea to ask her to slow down so the message has a chance to sink in. I know she'd love it if you would talk about how this applies in her life."

Some of the parents looked at Kim as if she was speaking a foreign language. They had gotten so caught up in the race that they had lost sight of the true goal.

As disciplers, we can get caught in the same trap. We do discipleship for the wrong motives: the need to be needed, the need to be appreciated, the need to be important, the need to feel wanted, the need to impress someone or prove something, the need to be powerful (or overpower others), the need to live up to unfulfilled expectations, or the inability to say no when we're asked to be involved.

> " We do discipleship as a matter of self-defense. We're not pouring into others; we're filling up ourselves. We're not standing strong, poised to risk the perils of the journey; we're cowering in a corner, willing to join someone's quest only if it has no downside for us. "

We do discipleship as a matter of self-defense. We're not pouring into others; we're filling up ourselves. We're not standing strong, poised to risk the perils of the journey; we're cowering in a corner, willing to join someone's quest only if it has no downside for us.

The next signpost we'll discuss—risk—is the remedy for such timid companionship. Whether we do one-on-one discipleship, lead small groups, or pastor churches, we'll be effective disciplers only when we're willing to model an attitude of risk for those we disciple. We'll be willing to risk when we see ourselves as loved and accepted, regardless of performance, numbers, accomplishments, or failures lingering from the past.

The gospel says our identity is not contingent upon merit, skill, charisma, or charm. The gospel says grace gives us dignity and worth. And the gospel says none of our attempts at earning that grace (or acceptance and approval) through performance, technique, spectacular feats, or clever management, get us any further ahead. Grace is freely offered, not earned. That's why it's called grace!

The gospel says our worth is based solely on who Jesus is and on what he has done for us through his life, death, and resurrection; and that we can be effective precisely because we don't have to take ourselves too seriously. Because grace takes us seriously, we don't have to impress, prove, or overpower.

To a postmodern young adult, this is great news! So many in this generation feel they don't measure up to what the church—or any authority—expects of them. But because of grace, what others expect of us simply carries no weight! One of the great truths in Christians' identification with Christ is that we have nothing to lose.

Paul declared to the Galatians, "I have been crucified with Christ and I no longer live, but Christ lives in me" (2:20). He also told the Philippians that only one thing mattered—that "Christ will be exalted in my body, whether by life or by death" (1:20). Then immediately, in the next verse, he captures the reason Christians are free to be risk takers: "For to me, to live is Christ and to die is gain" (1:21).

We have nothing to lose: Loss of reputation only makes us identify more with Christ. Loss of friends only makes us more dependent on Christ and his body. Even death for Christians is victory. That truth enabled young

QUEST

EXPERIENCE

With your fellow travelers, choose one of the following activities and do it.

1. Go somewhere in your city and share your spiritual journey with a stranger.

2. Go to a dirty part of your city and spend two hours cleaning it up.

3. Go to a needy part of your city and meet a need.

Then discuss your experience.

- What happened?

- Describe the people you met. What were their reactions to you?

- At any point did you feel like a failure? Explain. Why is this feeling normal?

- In what ways was this experience risky?

- How did that risk make you feel?

- How does risk strengthen faith?

Cassie Bernall, murdered at Columbine High School, to risk her life when facing down her killer. Remember what the missionary Jim Elliot wrote in his diary: "He is no fool who gives what he cannot keep to gain that which he cannot lose."[1]

We are free. Jesus said that if he would make us free, we would be free indeed (John 8:36). Whenever the challenge to risk arises, we might ask ourselves, What would be the worst possible thing that could happen if I take this risk? At times we might trace our line of reasoning back to "I

QUESTions

- As a Christian, how do you define success? failure? risk?

could lose my life." That's certainly one of the most dramatic possibilities, but even then we are winners. We have nothing to lose, not even life.

Cassie Bernall risked her life, as did the Apostle Paul and Jim Elliot. But God seldom asks his followers to risk their lives as these few did. Most of us tend to face risks more like the one faced by a young man from Frontline named Clay. He wanted to make a difference in kids' lives but had no real background, no team of helpers, no real training. Just a desire to make a difference and a willingness to risk failure.

"So many in this generation feel they don't measure up to what the church—or any authority—expects of them. But because of grace, what others expect of us simply carries no weight! One of the great truths in Christians' identification with Christ is that we have nothing to lose."

Clay started a mentoring program for kids of single parents and poured himself into it. He tried to get Frontline to join him and own it, and he was successful for a while. But for the most part, he worked alone to fulfill his sense of mission. Finally, after working in obscurity for a year, he stopped. On the surface, the program seemed like a failure. Yet nothing could be further from the truth. Week after week, single parents in our church whose kids were touched by Clay tell me what a huge difference he made in their children's faith. Clay's risk, which seemed like a failure, continues to pay dividends in the changed lives of children.

Are you a risk taker? Probably not. Most of us quite naturally pull back from risk. We actually like the idea of risk, but we'd rather experience it vicariously. So we pay to watch others take chances, and buy tickets to watch someone else risking. Or we turn on the TV, sit back in our chairs, and watch extreme sports.

Risk takers are often entertainers for the rest of us. For most people, life is primarily about creating safety and predictability. One of the greatest human pursuits is the pursuit of comfort zones. The problem with pursuing safety and predictability, however, is that the result is often terribly boring. If we never risked, we would never move away from home, find a job, ask for a raise, make a friend, or fall in love. The accounts in Scriptures abound of men and women who were risk takers. They range from the famous, such as Abraham, to the obscure, Epaphroditus.

> " Are you a risk taker? Probably not. Most of us quite naturally pull back from risk. We actually like the idea of risk, but we'd rather experience it vicariously. So we pay to watch others take chances, and buy tickets to watch someone else risking. Or we turn on the TV, sit back in our chairs, and watch extreme sports. "

About Abraham we are told: "By faith Abraham, when called to go to a place he would later receive as his inheritance, obeyed and went, even though he did not know where

QUEStions

- Are you a risk taker? Why or why not?

- What has been your experience with taking risks in life? in faith?

he was going" (Hebrews 11:8). One item the writer of Hebrews didn't mention was that Abraham was seventy-five years old when he set out for the Promised Land.

The little-known Epaphroditus was a messenger to the Apostle Paul from the church at Philippi. He was sent by the Philippian church to Rome to help Paul, who was in prison.

Epaphroditus was a risk taker. Yet, interestingly, Epaphroditus' mission in the eyes of Paul was not a raving success. He had come to Rome to serve Paul, but instead became ill, homesick, and distressed that his loved ones in Philippi were worried about him. This turn of events caused Paul to have anxiety over the situation. So instead of being a help to Paul, Epaphroditus was actually a burden.

Paul decided to send Epaphroditus back to his people. Yet look what Paul has to say about this man: "But I think it is necessary to send back to you Epaphroditus, my brother, fellow worker and fellow soldier, who is also your messenger, whom you sent to take care of my needs…Welcome him in the Lord with great joy, and honor men like him, because he almost died for the work of Christ, risking his life to make up for the help you could not give me" (Philippians 2:25, 29-30).

QUEStions

- Make a list of people who took risks in the Bible—you may want to read all of Hebrews 11.

- How did they end up? Were they successes or failures?

The phrase Paul uses to say Epaphroditus risked his life is a Greek idiom that literally means "he staked his life on a throw of the dice." Paul makes it sound like Epaphroditus' ministry had been a genuine success. We know differently. Yet Paul saw something that was far more important than success. He saw a man of obedience and faithfulness. God asks nothing more of you or me.

The way to help young adults on the quest for Christ is to help them understand they have nothing to lose, and they have the freedom to fail. Then we can help them face discomfort and fear.

In Nehemiah 2, Nehemiah faces an agonizing situation. In verse 2 he writes, "I was very much afraid." He had good reason to be: Unless a person was physically ill, to enter the presence of the king with a sad face was a capital crime. Nehemiah was not ill, but he decided that it was time to let the king see how he really felt.

The moment was tense. Nehemiah faced an agonizing situation: Either he remained in his world of secluded weeping and mourning, or he had to put his life on the line. The situation is clearly one that placed him outside his comfort zone.

Perhaps the ultimate example of someone being forced outside his comfort zone is Jesus struggling before the Father in the Garden of Gethsemane. He faced the cross. And one thing is certain about a cross—it has no comfort zones.

Yes, the cross is the ultimate illustration of how risk forces us out of our comfort zones. And God does call some of his followers to specific times of risking in their lives. But for most of us, our struggles will not be as dramatic as was that of Nehemiah before the king or that of Jesus sweating blood in the Garden of Gethsemane. Our struggles are more likely to be like those of a young adult named Jim.

When Jim moved to Washington, D.C., the atmosphere of Frontline was supportive and nonthreatening. It was just what he needed during his time of transition. He got involved in leadership in small groups. He was learning the important element of risk by allowing himself to be stretched.

He said: "By nature, I am not an extrovert and taking any leadership was a definite test of faith for me. Through Frontline leadership I learned that in order to grow, I had to step out in faith and not use my excuses, but rely on the Lord. I eventually became the leader of small groups at Frontline. There's no way you could have told me five years earlier that I could have done this."

QUESTions

- What kinds of "risks" could you "plan" for those you are discipling?

- What is there to gain through experiencing risk?

- What is there to lose?

A friend of mine likes to ask a trick question: "Which of God's prohibitions do you suppose occurs most frequently in Scripture?" People immediately think of thou shalt not lie, steal, murder, and so on. But remember, this is a trick question. The answer is not any of the "thou shalt nots" but rather it is "fear not." Yes, of all the negative commands of Scripture, "fear not" is the one repeated most often.

Well, Nehemiah did fear. But God saw him through. After all, the worst that could have happened was that he lost his life. Yet even if he had, he was still a winner because his God is Lord over death.

Nehemiah could possibly have failed in his attempt to get the wall rebuilt. But we know that success is not the issue. What is important is that in his attempt, Nehemiah was faithful to his Lord.

Nehemiah was where we need to be from time to time—out of our comfort zones. And when we are, if God has led us there, we can relax because over and over again we're encouraged by God's Word to "fear not."

> We can encourage young adults to take risks because
> - neither we nor they have anything to lose,
> - it's OK to fail, and
> - faith equips us to handle discomfort and fear.

Risk forces us away from ourselves and demands that we depend upon our Lord. And our dependence upon him enables us to serve him outside our normal comfort zones.

People who risk realize it's OK to fail. God is not primarily interested in success, rather he is interested in faithfulness and effort.

Several years ago one of our staff named Courtney had the big idea to create a discipleship model based on the program *Road Rules* from MTV. This approach had a dynamic that we all liked very much. It could have flopped. But that wouldn't have diminished the faithfulness of Courtney and everyone involved in this risky venture.

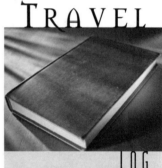

TRAVEL LOG

Later in this book we give you a brief description of how to set up an IntenCity program, the program Courtney designed. See page 183.

FREEDOM TO FAIL

Assisting others in their Christ formation is about becoming the encourager, the one who shares the good news of God's grace. Our theology of Christ formation, then, begins with what God says about us (that is, the gospel of grace) and not a generic lecture from God to us about discipleship. You see, the purpose of theology is to teach us about our relationship with God and consequently to liberate us to become more of who we were created to be. It's not just information and material necessary to study for some test on life. Theology is not just God's how-to manual or divine *CliffsNotes* on better living.

The more comfortable we become with the role of God's grace in the life of the one we disciple, the more we'll relax and let him or her struggle and fail along the way. We keep too close an eye on the bottom line. We need to move people from feeling the pressure of performance. We need to learn to sit back and take pleasure in the unfolding work of the Holy Spirit in the lives of those we disciple.

One of my mentors was Bruce Larson, the senior pastor of a church in Seattle where I served. I worked closely with another young pastor, and the two of us drove Bruce crazy with our antics. But Bruce rarely if ever criticized. He watched, guided, chatted, and listened as the Holy Spirit worked in us. The harshest thing I remember him saying was when he turned to my friend and said,

QUE8tions

- Who has given you freedom to fail?

- How has that affected your faith? your understanding of God?

"John, you have such a gift for coloring outside the lines!" Bruce didn't tie his reputation to my growth or John's, he provided the environment of nurture and acceptance that allowed us to grow.

Jesus provided that same kind of environment. Take a look at the foot-washing story in John 13:1-5.

> It was just before the Passover Feast. Jesus knew that the time had come for him to leave this world and go to the Father. Having loved his own who were in the world, he now showed them the full extent of his love.
>
> The evening meal was being served, and the devil had already prompted Judas Iscariot, son of Simon, to betray Jesus. Jesus knew that the Father had put all things under his power, and that he had come from God and was returning to God; so he got up

from the meal, took off his outer clothing, and wrapped a towel around his waist. After that, he poured water into a basin and began to wash his disciples' feet, drying them with the towel that was wrapped around him.

Jesus was able to have compassion on his disciples and risk rejection because his identity was not dependent upon his ministry—or public opinion, year-end reports, media re-sponse, board pressure, or memories of past failures. He felt free to fail. As a matter of fact, one wonders if he ever lost sight of the fact that he was sent here for the express purpose of "failing" by death on the cross.

QUE8†ions

If you really want to take a risk, tell your fellow travelers about your greatest failure.

- What is the one thing you're struggling with right now?

- How does a nurturing environment affect our experience of risk?

We can help people feel free to fail by providing nurturing environments. As Paul says, "Who are you to judge someone else's servant? To his own master he stands or falls. And he will stand, for the Lord is able to make him stand" (Romans 14:4). This text in Romans talks about our tendency to set ourselves up as someone else's master. We become critic, expert, judge, and jury for those around us. It's as if the Holy Spirit is too busy, so we think we'll take a crack at the people-changing business. It's understandable. It stems again from our taking ourselves too seriously.

If it's true that we aren't responsible for others and that our identity is not dependent upon their choices, being fixed, or changing, then we are free to create an environment of nurture where their Master, Christ, can develop them. Maybe, just maybe, we can begin to see them with a sense of wonder and expectancy.

We can see beyond the immediate to the potential as Jesus did in Luke 7:36-50.

Now one of the Pharisees invited Jesus to have dinner with him, so he went to the Pharisee's house and reclined at the table.

When a woman who had lived a sinful life in that town learned that Jesus was eating at the Pharisee's house, she brought an alabaster jar of perfume, and as she stood behind him at his feet weeping, she began to wet his feet with her tears. Then she wiped them with her hair, kissed them and poured perfume on them.

When the Pharisee who had invited him saw this, he said to himself, "If this man were a prophet, he would know who is touching him and what kind of woman she is—that she is a sinner."

Jesus answered him, "Simon, I have something to tell you."

"Tell me, teacher," he said.

"Two men owed money to a certain moneylender. One owed him five hundred denarii, and the other fifty. Neither of them had the money to pay him back, so he canceled the debts of both. Now which of them will love him more?"

Simon replied, "I suppose the one who had the bigger debt canceled."

"You have judged correctly," Jesus said.

Then he turned toward the woman and said to Simon, "Do you see this woman? I came into your house. You did not give me any water for my feet, but she wet my feet with her tears and wiped them with her hair. You did not give me a kiss, but this woman, from the time I entered, has not stopped kissing my feet. You did not put oil on my head, but she has poured perfume on my feet. Therefore, I tell you, her many sins have been forgiven—for she loved much. But he who has been forgiven little loves little."

Then Jesus said to her, "Your sins are forgiven."

QUEStions

Jesus gave people the freedom to grow. His ministry was not taken from a prepublished discipleship method. He saw people as unique, as individuals.

- How is the freedom to fail the same as the freedom to grow?

And he always saw beyond the immediate to the "more" they could become. In this story from the gospel of Luke, Jesus gives a prostitute the permission to believe that she is more than the sum of her parts (sinner, prostitute, woman from the wrong side of the tracks). What did Jesus do for this woman? He created an environment for her growth. He nurtured her growth. A nurturer does not see people as they are, but sees them as they shall become.

NURTURING THE NURTURER

Just like those Awana parents, we must struggle against the temptation to turn nurture back on ourselves. We must fight the tide that pulls us away from the growth of the other and toward attention for ourselves. Yet we, too, need nurture. We don't disciple others because we've somehow arrived at some place that converts us from student to teacher. We, too, are in process. We're still learning. We need God's continuing supply of grace as much as the disciples around us.

> " We don't disciple others because we've somehow arrived at some place that converts us from student to teacher. We, too, are in process. We're still learning. We need God's continuing supply of grace as much as the disciples around us. "

Again, Jesus is our example here. Simply put, Jesus could care for others because he took care of himself. He made sure he was regularly in a place where he was being nurtured. And this was a source of consistent irritation for his followers and his critics: "Why isn't Jesus always available when we need him? And why does he never do things the way we would expect? And why isn't he being the kind of Messiah that our tradition says that he should be? And why does he have so little regard for public opinion?"

It would be difficult for Jesus to live in modern America—Jesus was a publicist's nightmare! And is it no wonder that we—who are so worried about being "somebody" or being with somebody who is somebody or of being able to produce a stellar resume—have difficulty in the area of self-care. We are driven by public opinion, and we easily sacrifice who we are today for who we think we should be. We too easily believe that being important is better than being real.

What does it mean that Jesus practiced self-care? In today's jargon it means that he had boundaries. It means that he was not a victim to every whim of the adoring public (or, depending on its mood, the antagonistic public). It means that he

> " We are driven by public opinion, and we easily sacrifice who we are today for who we think we should be. We too easily believe that being important is better than being real. "

respected his limitations—he was, after all, human with all its implications of weariness, loneliness, and doubt. It means that he knew he needed a regular reminder that his identity was intact apart from the jobs and tasks

·QUEST

STORY

Kim, a very young new single mom, had not grown up in the church, but wanted to find good people her age. She heard of Frontline and showed up. She eventually realized she needed God in her life and committed her life to him. Soon after that she wanted to do something to make a difference, so playing from her weakness, she started a Bible Study with other young single moms. She said, "I never realized how much I would grow by being honest with some other single moms about how hard it is to be this age with a son. But I found a whole bunch of fellow journeyers."

he performed. It means that his sense of worth was not dependent upon needing to fix and rescue everyone around him.

It's no wonder that throughout the gospel record, we find Jesus regularly withdrawing to a "solitary place." Why? To pray. To practice self-care. To gain perspective. To be reminded that reality is more than just the line of people waiting to be healed, counseled, fixed, or stroked.

A lifestyle of self-care is a two-sided coin that includes both withdrawing and community. Withdrawing without community can easily lead to isolation. It's in community (to be distinguished from the general public) that we find regular encouragement, affirmation, and challenge in those areas of our lives that need to change.

In isolation our boundaries can be easily erased, and our identity is once again wed to our ability to perform and impress. We can only model risk when our lives contain a balance of community and withdrawal.

WEAK SAFETY

There's a position on a football team called the weak safety. This player's job is a vital one. When he doesn't do his job, the game can be lost. I've always been struck by the juxtaposition of the term. Weakness and safety as part of the same package. Doesn't that speak to our position in the Kingdom?

The fact is, we're a mess. We wouldn't need a savior if we weren't. You wouldn't need a book on discipling others if you weren't. And that's OK; God's strength is shown best by our weakness. So while taking care of ourselves is important, allowing God to work through our brokenness is more important.

QUE8†ions

- If you knew that you couldn't fail, what would you do for God?

- If those you're discipling knew they couldn't fail, what would they do for God?

- What specific things can you do to encourage risk?

"My grace is sufficient for you, for my power is made perfect in weakness." Therefore I will boast all the more gladly about my weaknesses, so that Christ's power may rest on me" (2 Corinthians 12:9).

We all feel this need to be strong, to be impressive and powerful, to be above any suspicion of weakness. The irony is that God's grace is reflected only through those who have experienced brokenness, forgiveness, and renewal.

QUE8†ions

- How does our failure help us serve others?

- Are you willing to risk failure to be a true servant?

Henri Nouwen says our call is to be "wounded healers." What does that mean? It means that God's power—to heal, to reconcile, to care—is manifested not in our strengths, skills, techniques, or cleverness, but in our weaknesses—brokenness, pain, vulnerability, and even our failures).

God reflects his love through us in ways that we would least expect. The Scriptures give us this assurance about the value of our weakness.

Praise be to the God and Father of our Lord Jesus Christ, the
Father of compassion and the God of all comfort, who comforts
us in all our troubles, so that we can comfort those in any trouble with the comfort we ourselves have received from God. For
just as the sufferings of Christ flow over into our lives, so also
through Christ our comfort overflows. If we are distressed, it is
for your comfort and salvation; if we are comforted, it is for your
comfort, which produces in you patient endurance of the same
sufferings we suffer. And our hope for you is firm, because we
know that just as you share in our sufferings, so also you share in
our comfort (2 Corinthians 1:3-7).

As I mentioned, my daughters were Awana Club members for several
years. When Jessa was in kindergarten, she'd been in Awana for three years
and had been discipled by loving leaders to understand something of her
brokenness and God's grace.

In April of Jessa's kindergarten year, two students at Columbine High
School, not forty miles from our house, shot and killed twelve school-
mates and a teacher before killing themselves. In all, fifteen people died.
The two had killed thirteen. We tried to keep the horror of the events
from our young girls, but within a few days it was clear they'd heard
enough at school that we needed to address what had happened. We had
heard in the news that there was a tremendous outpouring of grief and
love in the form of memorial shrines that had been established sponta-
neously by thousands of visitors to the massacre site.

Thinking our girls needed to be assured that God's love abides even in
times of great evil, we took a family trip to the school. With hundreds of
others, we slowly made our way along fence lines adorned with teddy
bears, notes, floral bouquets, and other tokens of grief and love. Soon we
joined a long line that had formed to snake past fifteen crosses that had
been erected secretly one night on a nearby hillock.

During the days immediately after the appearance of the fifteen crosses,
the newspapers and radio call-in shows had been filled with debate and no
little outrage at the appearance and number of crosses. Many argued the
crosses should be taken down altogether. Many more argued that the two

representing the killers should be razed. Standing in line, we discussed the current debate with our girls and wondered what they thought. Six-year-old Jessa thought about what she knew of God's grace and answered with conviction. "I think all fifteen crosses should stay. It says in Romans 5:8 that Christ died for us while we were still sinners, and I know he died for those boys, since they're sinners like us." When we allow God's grace to flow through us to those we disciple in spite of our woundedness, they become fellow agents of that grace.

NOTES

1   Elisabeth Elliott, *The Shadow of the Almighty* (San Francisco: Harper and Row, 1958), 108.

Signpost Five

HOPE

> *"'For I know the plans I have for you,' declares the Lord, 'plans to prosper you and not to harm you, plans to give you hope and a future.'"*
>
> –Jeremiah 29:11

Like most people, my (Rich's) thoughts were a tangled ball of twine in the hours and days following the attacks of September 11, 2001. I don't remember having many answers in those days, but I sure had a thousand questions. How many are dead? How many are hurt? Will there be more attacks? As the hours turned into days, my questions changed. Why did this happen? What might have prevented it?

Soon I made the shift from what had happened to what might happen. How are we to recover from this? How can we be more aware of danger? What can we do to promote peace? What good does the future hold in light of September 11? Our political and community leaders found ways to see past the events and bolster our hope for a better future.

> "In many ways, tragedy begets hope. Times of war, devastating illness, or personal tragedy cause us to reflect on the things that really matter. We look beyond the situation at hand to the hope for a better future. We recognize that without hope, we'll be cast adrift by our circumstances."

In many ways, tragedy begets hope. Times of war, devastating illness, or

personal tragedy cause us to reflect on the things that really matter. We look beyond the situation at hand to the hope for a better future. We recognize that without hope, we'll be cast adrift by our circumstances.

Dr. Viktor Frankl, an Austrian psychiatrist who was a prisoner in Auschwitz and other concentration camps during WWII, wrote about the power of hope in his book *Man's Search for Meaning:* "The prisoner who had lost faith in the future—his future—was doomed. With his loss of belief in the future, he also lost his spiritual hold; he let himself decline and become subject to mental and physical decay."[1]

QUESTIONS

- What is hope?

- How does hope affect your life?

Hope for the future relies on vision. You find the hope to get through cancer because you have a vision of the day when you'll be healthy again. You find hope when you can see beyond September 2001 to a better September in the future. The Bible talks a lot about the importance of having vision. As a matter of fact, these days, just about everyone talks about having vision.

As Leonard Sweet says, "Fifty years ago, if you admitted you had a 'vision' the people in white coats would come and take you away. Now everyone has a 'vision,' and those who don't are taken away. You can't run for garbage collector these days without a vision. Every corporation has one. Every individual has one. Every church has one."[2]

WHEN VISION FAILS

But the hope born of vision to see beyond present circumstances is no weapon against the sort of hopelessness that characterizes many postmodern young adults. Hopelessness felt by the postmodern is actually a profound sense of meaninglessness. What is the meaning of life—of my life— if there is no objective reality? If I am the sole arbiter of right and wrong, of good and evil, of beauty and chaos, of truth and fiction, then true meaning has no foundation. Try as I may, I can find no true foothold for

QUE8†

EXPERIENCE

Meet with your fellow travelers. Have each traveler mold something out of clay. Before starting, have each person describe a vision for what he or she wants to create. Afterward, discuss whether your sculptures matched your vision.

- How is this experience similar to the disillusionment that occurs when real life doesn't match up to our expectations?

- Describe how people lose hope.

- How can the quest for Christ restore hope?

- As a discipler, how can you facilitate the regaining of hope?

my existence. I can't deny I exist, but neither can I find a reason for my existence.

It's this sense of meaninglessness that characterizes many of the postmodern seekers I encounter. A handsome young man named Alex is a good example. I met Alex at one of our young adult meetings. On the surface, Alex has a lot going for him. Aside from good looks, he's got a lot of other assets. For one thing, he's got a great job. He works for an entertainment concern and gets to rub elbows with many famous singers, actors, and athletes. His life is rather glamorous. It's also rather meaningless. Like many of his colleagues, Alex has coped by developing a pretty serious drug habit. In the fog of intoxication, he can temporarily ignore the hopelessness of a life without true meaning.

Viktor Frankl observed that prisoners who had family or loved ones to return to found a hope they could cling to in the camps. They knew they belonged to someone. They found hope in their identity. They found their identity in their relationship to those who loved them and awaited their return home.[3] This is what Alex needs to grasp if he's going to find hope. God, who made him, loves him and waits for him to return home.

QUE8†ions

- What is it that gives you a sense of meaning and purpose in life?

- What would your life be like if you didn't have that sense of purpose?

- What is life like for young adults plagued by a sense of meaninglessness?

Is Alex an atheist? No. Alex is quite open to the idea and even the person of God. Alex is quite spiritual as a matter of fact. He sometimes searches the Bible for answers to life's questions, he attends occasional church functions, he might even think of himself as a Christian. But he has yet to make the connection between his life and the love Jesus has extended to him through his death.

> " But the hope born of vision to see beyond present circumstances is no weapon against the sort of hopelessness that characterizes many postmodern young adults. Hopelessness felt by the postmodern is actually a profound sense of meaninglessness. "

Alex is not alone in this. Leonard Sweet explains that "Postmoderns are anti-religious but deeply spiritual. Postmodern culture is filled with day trippers asking for direction, some with feet on the ground, others stuck in the mud, still others with heads in the clouds—but all scouring the horizon for hope, wonder, and a way out of the mazes of aimless living."[4] How then shall we instill hope in a spiritually-oriented but disillusioned young adult like Alex? Since hope is one of the signposts along our quest, we recognize that it must be a necessary component of our journey with Alex. Where does

QUESTions

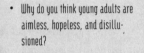

• Why do you think young adults are aimless, hopeless, and disillusioned?

• How does hope figure into the quest for Christ?

Alex look to find that hope?

Shall we point him to one of the discipleship programs at church? Probably not. You know what they say about leading a horse to water. Our church offers many fine discipleship programs, but Alex is unlikely to participate in any of them until he begins the process of changing how he thinks. This is where imagination again becomes important. Alex will be willing to participate in a discipleship program only after he has enough vision to imagine a life of intimacy with God. That vision will only be sparked when Alex can see, even experience, true intimacy with God lived out in the lives of believers like me.

> " Our job in instilling hope in their lives is to help them see the truth about God. This is what Jesus did over and over again. "

What most people believe about God they have either derived from their life experiences or from other people's opinions. Our job in instilling hope in their lives is to help them see the truth about God. This is what Jesus did over and over again. The religious leaders of Jesus' day had reduced God to a list of rules and regulations. They had established religion instead of a relationship with God. Jesus' life on earth cleared up the myth of religiosity to those who had ears to hear. Unfortunately, this was not a lesson learned once and for all. Today's young adults tend to believe four misconceptions that hinder them from seeing Christ as the source of their hope:

QUEStions

- What myths about God do you see in young adult thinking?

- Where do those myths come from?

- How can you help young adults replace those myths with a more accurate picture of God?

Myth: God is unreasonable.
Truth: God's reasons are beyond our knowing, but are essentially compassionate.

Young adults have grown up in a world that seems to make no sense. How could a reasonable God let their parents get divorced? How could God let so many of their siblings be aborted? How could a reasonable God allow AIDS? We need to help people like Alex see that God is a caring God and if he is withholding something or allowing evil, it is no indictment of his essential nature, which is loving and compassionate. "[God] is good to everyone, and his compassion is intertwined with everything he does" (Psalm 145:9, *The Living Bible*).

Myth: God is unreliable.
Truth: God is consistent.

Where was God when these young adults were left home alone as children while their parents worked? Where was God when Columbine happened? Where was God when the World Trade Center was attacked? People think they can't trust God either because they misunderstand life's circumstances or because they project their own father image on God. But the Bible describes God as consistently good and consistently loving.

"God will never go back on his promises" (Romans 11:29b, *TLB*).

"My God is changeless in his love for me" (Psalm 59:10a, *TLB*).

Myth: God is unconcerned.
Truth: God is caring.

When Alex's brother died of a drug overdose, where was God? When his parents moved for the tenth time, where was God? We need to help people like Alex see that they matter to God.

"Not one sparrow can fall to the ground without your Father knowing it" (Matthew 10:29, *TLB*).

Myth: God is unpleasable.
Truth: God is gracious.

Young adults often feel that God demands an impossible level of perfection and then severely punishes any who don't achieve that perfection.

But the message of Scripture is that God is so gracious that he provides forgiveness of all sin to any who want it and believe in him.

"[God] has accepted you because of what the Lord Jesus Christ and the Spirit of our God have done for you" (1 Corinthians 6:11b, *TLB*).

"Long ago, even before he made the world, God chose us to be his very own through what Christ would do for us; he decided then to make us holy in his eyes, without a single fault—we who stand before him covered with his love" (Ephesians 1:4, *TLB*).

REGAINING HOPE

If I thought God were unreasonable, unreliable, unpleasable, and unconcerned, I'd lose hope, too. But because I know he's giving, gracious, caring, and consistent, and that I belong to him and am the beneficiary of those traits, I have tremendous hope!

But people like Alex understand neither God's character nor their own identity within that character. The way to instill hope in others is to help them rethink their concept of self and God. Our job as disciple makers, as guides on the quest, is to help them understand their true identity in Christ.

The starting point of the postmodern young adult's quest for Christ is coming to the understanding that he or she is made in the image of God—this is true identity. This truth goes to the core of what young adults struggle with because understanding our identity in Christ is what gives life meaning. Failing to understand this basic truth, the hopeless young adult searches for identity in fruitless pursuits: the perfect job, the perfect relationship, the perfect house or car. When these things don't materialize, and they never do, the young adult feels further imprisoned by his or her own sense of insignificance.

QUE8tions

- How do you see young adults pursuing things that will ultimately rob them of hope?

- How will understanding their true identity restore their hope?

In prison Viktor Frankl could hold on to hope for release because he knew there were people who awaited his release. He knew he mattered to caring, concerned family members. The problem for many young adults lost in hopelessness is that they do not know that a loving Father awaits their return to true intimacy with him. Rather than long for an intimate relationship with a caring Father, these young adults long to meet obligations set for them by their own imaginations or by those around them. *If I'll only do thus and such,* they reason, *I'll know who I am and why I matter.*

This longing to fulfill obligations set by themselves or others becomes their master. They become enslaved by a need

❝ The problem for many young adults lost in hopelessness is that they do not know that a loving Father awaits their return to true intimacy with him. ❞

to perform, to achieve, to accomplish. When they fail, they are sucked even deeper into hopelessness and are further beholden to a cruel and nameless master.

But God desires us to be wholly and fully alive. Disillusioned young adults like my friend Alex have somehow missed that promise. As a result, they feel pulled in various directions by many different owners or masters. As we befriend the Alexes in our lives and walk with them on their journey toward intimacy with God, we can help them turn away from false masters only by demonstrating our own submission to the one true master and by helping them discover his promises to them. Promises like these:

"It is for freedom that Christ has set us free. Stand firm, then, and do not let yourselves be burdened again by a yoke of slavery" (Galatians 5:1).

"Don't let the world around you squeeze you into its own mould, but let God re-make you so that your whole attitude of mind is changed" (Romans 12:2, New Testament in Modern English/Phillips).

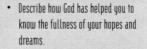

QUESTions

- Describe how God has helped you to know the fullness of your hopes and dreams.

- What would happen if young adults understood the abundant life they could have in God?

It's so important that young adults truly understand God's loving and trustworthy nature because it's only then that young adults will be able to begin to regain their hope. An experience with my daughters has helped me understand this.

My girls used to catch garter snakes in our back yard. I hate snakes, just as most people do. But my girls were little and hadn't yet developed any kind of snake phobia, so snake catching was a favorite pastime in the meadow behind the house. One day I was on my way to a meeting at which I was speaking. I had new clothes on and was feeling good about my appearance. My daughters were on the porch of our house with their latest reptilian friends. When they saw me, they held up the snakes for me to see through the sliding glass doors and yelled, "Hey, Dad, look at these!"

Now snakes react the way most humans and animals do when they're terrified—they wet themselves. This is an incredibly nasty event because the fluid runs down the arms of whoever happens to be holding the snake aloft. This had just occurred when my daughters realized I was leaving, and they decided to hug and kiss me goodbye. Now I had a choice: Did I reject them to keep the stench from the snake off me, or did I embrace them? At that last minute, I held out my arms and we hugged, smell and all. The rest of the day I carried to all my meetings a potent souvenir of my daughters' love.

This is similar to how God responds to us. He doesn't demand we come clean; he just asks us to come. He accepts us just as we are. Whereas the cruel master of unreachable expectations demands performance and perfection, our heavenly master, our Father, allows us to come just as we are, covered in the stench of our own poor choices.

The Bible contains a well-known story about a loving father and his own smelly son. The parable of the prodigal son offers insight to hopeless young

QUE8tions

Recall an experience from your own life that has helped you understand God's love.

• How did that experience change your relationship with God?

• How can you help young adults recognize God at work around them?

adults searching for meaning, and offers three lessons that will help young adults regain hope in God. Let's review the text.

> There was a man who had two sons. The younger one said to his father, "Father, give me my share of the estate." So he divided his property between them.
>
> Not long after that, the younger son got together all he had, set off for a distant country and there squandered his wealth in wild living. After he had spent everything, there was a severe famine in that whole country, and he began to be in need. So he went and hired himself out to a citizen of that country, who sent him to his fields to feed pigs. He longed to fill his stomach with the pods that the pigs were eating, but no one gave him anything.
>
> When he came to his senses, he said, "How many of my father's hired men have food to spare, and here I am starving to death! I will set out and go back to my father and say to him: Father, I have sinned against heaven and against you. I am no longer worthy to be called your son; make me like one of your hired men." So he got up and went to his father (Luke 15:11-20).

Lesson 1: The first lesson for young adults in this parable is the importance of confessing, admitting the hopelessness of one's current situation. The prodigal son made an accurate confession of his own failings. He stopped and said, "I was wrong." Confession is simply admitting what you have done wrong and taking responsibility for it. It's acknowledging that you've headed down the wrong path on your quest and correcting your mistake so you get back on track.

> " Whereas the cruel master of unreachable expectations demands performance and perfection, our heavenly master, our Father, allows us to come just as we are, covered in the stench of our own poor choices. "

Ephesians 5:1-2a says it this way: "Be imitators of God, therefore, as dearly loved children and live a life of love, just as Christ loved us and gave himself up for us." Is this hard to do? On the surface it appears to be, but we have God's promises: "I can do all things through Christ who strengthens me" (Philippians 4:13, NKJ); "Therefore, if anyone is in Christ, he is a new creation; the old has gone, the new has come!" (2 Corinthians 5:17); "There is now no condemnation for those who are in Christ Jesus" (Romans 8:1); "And we know that in all things God works for the good of those who love him, who have been called according to his purpose" (Romans 8:28).

QUES†ions

- How does confession begin the journey toward regaining hope?

- How can you help young adults to come to the point of confession? Are some methods better than others?

Lesson 2: Once young adults are able to admit the hopelessness of their situations, they can move on to the second lesson in this parable: They can stop listening to the voices that insist on perfect performance and start listening to the loving voice of a Father who calls them to his side and back into fellowship. Let's look again at Luke 15 and see the father's response as the prodigal son approached the house.

> But the father said to his servants, "Quick! Bring the best robe and put it on him. Put a ring on his finger and sandals on his feet.

Bring the fattened calf and kill it. Let's have a feast and celebrate. For this son of mine was dead and is alive again; he was lost and is found." So they began to celebrate (Luke 15:22-24).

The message to the prodigal son is "You are loved no matter where you've been." That's the kind of love God offers to us. I have watched in wonder as my friend John loves his son Matt. It would be understandable for John to give up on his wayward son, but never once have I seen him do that; he just keeps loving. Matt has gone through some tough times. And every time he calls his dad, John says in essence, "Call out the band; get the fattened calf." You know what that message conveys? It conveys that John loves Matt just because…That's God's message to us. He loves us just because—he embraces us because of his grace.

QUE8tions

- Why are young adults reluctant to accept the truth of God's love for them?

- What does it take to convince them that what God says is true?

Let me paraphrase Luke 15. The prodigal went to his father and said, "You're taking forever to die, so I need your money now. I can't wait until you die. Give me your money now." The father agreed for reasons no one but he understood.

The son took all that money, went to a distant land, and partied with abandon. After all of his money was gone and his friends went away, there was an economic downturn and a famine. He ended up with no place to stay and nothing to eat.

Finally, the kid said, "You know what? I have really fouled up. I am no longer worthy to be called my father's son. I have sinned against heaven and earth." He came to his senses and admitted his hopelessness. That kid figured out exactly what he deserved. He sorted out what justice was in his situation and concluded that his behavior warranted forfeiting his role as his father's son. His behavior warranted his father shunning him for the rest of his life.

He thought, "I screwed up big time. I've sinned against heaven and against earth, against my father and against my family. I know what I deserve—separation from my family for the rest of my life.

"But you know what? Maybe, maybe if I go home and own up to what I've done and admit what I deserve, maybe my dad will give me a little mercy." So he headed for home knowing he deserved justice, but hoping he'd be shown just a little mercy.

> " The truth is when we hear God say, 'I love you,' what we are hearing God say is 'Come into a saving relationship with me.' It's what it means to become a Christian, to hear the voice of a new master. "

As he went down the road, he saw his dad. The first thing he said was, "Dad, I know what I deserve! I have sinned against you. I have sinned against heaven. I am no longer worthy to be called your son."

But his dad surprised him. Before the son could even make the plea, "Would you give me a bed in with the hired hands?" his dad poured grace all over him.

His dad said, "I, too, know what you deserve. And I know what you hope for—my mercy. But I'm going to do one step better than mercy."

He wrapped his arms around the kid and said, "Welcome home! I'm so glad to see you. I'm going to kill the fattened calf. I'm going to put a ring on your finger, new sandals on your feet. We're going to throw the biggest party this family has ever experienced!"

And then the father poured on grace after grace after grace. He said, "You're going to come back and live in the main house. You're going to be my son. I love you."

Grace boggles the mind.

The truth is when we hear God say, "I love you," what we are hearing God say is "Come into a saving relationship with me." It's what it means to become a Christian, to hear the voice of a new master.

QUEStions

- How can you help young adults place their trust in the Truth?

"Ultimately, all of those masters to which [we have sold our] identity will die, or rust, or pass away and leave [us] empty. But God's gift of his love never fails: It remains constant when all else is unstable, and it will last through eternity."[5]

Lesson 3: The third lesson for hopeless young adults is to learn to place one's trust in the Truth and not in feelings. Let's continue in Luke 15.

> Meanwhile, the older son was in the field. When he came near the house, he heard music and dancing. So he called one of the servants and asked him what was going on. "Your brother has come," he replied, "and your father has killed the fattened calf because he has him back safe and sound."
>
> The older brother became angry and refused to go in. So his father went out and pleaded with him. But he answered his father, "Look! All these years I've been slaving for you and never disobeyed your orders. Yet you never gave me even a young goat so I could celebrate with my friends. But when this son of yours who has squandered your property with prostitutes comes home, you kill the fattened calf for him!

The brother made the same basic mistake as the prodigal son; he allowed his identity to be based on performance. Granted, the brother's behavior appears to have been exemplary, but performance is never the measure God uses as the basis for his acceptance of us. Discipleship is helping young adults overcome the temptation to rely on feelings rather than their true identity in Christ.

> " Performance is never the measure God uses as the basis for his acceptance of us. "

Scripture speaks to this temptation in several places. In Mark 9:23, Jesus says to a man, "Everything is possible for him who believes." The man replies, "I do believe; help me overcome my unbelief!" We can all relate to that dichotomy. Yes, we believe. But no, not entirely. The Apostle Paul spoke about his struggle to act on the things he knew to be true. He became so discouraged by this incongruity that he referred to himself as "chief" among sinners. In practical terms, we constantly wrestle with this. Very few of us simply decide to believe and that's that. There's a lot of acting on God's promises before we're convinced of their truthfulness.

SHARING HOPE

So how do you convey hope to the postmodern young adult who, through circumstance or simple force of habit, feels hopeless? We recognize that our fellow journeyers have not understood their true identity in Christ. I suggest you let these principles guide you:

1. Model your own hope. "Always be prepared to give an answer to everyone who asks you to give the reason for the hope that you have"

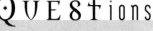

QUEStions

- What role does hope play in having the desire to be changed?

- How can you help young adults long for the transforming presence of God in their lives?

(1 Peter 3:15a). Live your life such that people notice the hope that you have. This means that a continual looking forward to the eternal world is not, as some modern people think, a form of escapism or wishful thinking, but one of the things a Christian is meant to do.

It doesn't mean that we are to leave the present world as it is. If you read history, you'll find the Christians who did the most for the present world were those who thought most of the next world. It's because Christians have largely ceased to think of the other world that they have become so ineffective in this. There's an adage that says, "Aim at heaven and you will get the earth thrown in. Aim at earth and you will get neither." We must always model an attitude that shows our focus is on the kingdom of God and his righteousness (Matthew 6:33).

> " ...a continual looking forward to the eternal world is not, as some modern people think, a form of escapism or wishful thinking, but one of the things a Christian is meant to do. "

2. Be secure in your true identity. Our security is neither in this world nor the things of this world. And it's precisely this matter of security that will instill hope in others, especially during times of personal doubt. Romans 15:13 says, "May the God of hope fill you with all joy and peace as you trust in him, so that you may overflow with hope by the power of the Holy Spirit."

3. Demonstrate God's power over your old sin nature. We have hope in the present because through Christ we are no longer slaves to sin. Romans 6:6 says, "Your old evil desires were nailed to the cross with him; that part of you that loves to sin was crushed and fatally wounded, so that your sin-loving body is no longer under sin's control, no longer needs to be a slave to sin; for when you are dead-ened to sin you are freed from all its allure and its power over you" *(TLB)*.

4. Help people see that God hasn't given

QUEStions

- Are these principles evident in your life? Why or why not?

- How would modeling these principles affect your discipleship efforts?

up on them and that he is concerned about them and searching for them. Scripture makes it clear that God is intent on redeeming people, loving them back into relationship with him.

TRAVEL LOG

If you've been following Christ for a long time, think back to the time when these ideas were new to you. As you disciple another, understand that these concepts will represent a shift in his or her thinking. Think of our metaphor of European travel. The first-time visitor to Europe will be thrown by all sorts of new concepts and encounters that will seem second nature to you, the seasoned traveler. As a thoughtful guide, you'll remember your first trip and will gently help the newcomer to correctly interpret these cultural shifts.

"Suppose one of you has a hundred sheep and loses one of them. Does he not leave the ninety-nine in the open country and go after the lost sheep until he finds it? And when he finds it, he joyfully puts it on his shoulders and goes home. Then he calls his friends and neighbors together and says, 'Rejoice with me; I have found my lost sheep.' I tell you that in the same way there will be more rejoicing in heaven over one sinner who repents than over ninety-nine righteous persons who do not need to repent" (Luke 15:4-7).

Understanding all these biblical truths ourselves is one thing. Helping the Alexes of the world to grasp them is another. I can't expect Alex to sit down with a fill-in-the-blank workbook and master these truths like he would a math lesson. I can't make Alex stay sober or arrange his work schedule to attend six weeks of Bible classes at church. I can't ask him to pluck up the courage to attend a small-group weekly Bible study in someone's home.

What I can do is model my hope for him as we meet at an all-night diner when he gets off work. I can model my hope in the phone calls I make to his cell phone sometimes several times a day. I can guide him toward answers when he's got questions. In short, remembering Viktor Frankl's observations, I can be a representative of the one who waits for him to return home when he is released from the prison of his own hopelessness.

NOTES

1. Viktor Frankl, *Man's Search for Meaning* (Boston, MA: Beacon Press, 1959), 117.
2. Leonard Sweet, *Aqua Church* (Loveland, CO: Group Publishing, Inc., 1999), 130.
3. Viktor Frankl, *Man's Search for Meaning.*
4. Leonard Sweet, *Aqua Church,* 41.
5. Rich Hurst, *Courage to Connect* (Colorado Springs, CO: Victor, 2002), 55.

SCRIPTURE

" Then something happened,
something that has changed
and transformed my life to the
present day. For the first time,
I discovered the Bible. "

—Dietrich Bonhoeffer

" The grass withers and the
flowers fall, but the word of our
God stands forever. "

—Isaiah 40:8

Unless you slept through the last ten years or so, you've seen the ubiquitous WWJD bracelet.

What a big deal this bracelet was for a time! Every school kid sported one. Business men and women wore them with suits. Teenagers fastened them to backpacks. Once it was obvious this thing had caught on, and there was money to be made, we started seeing the higher-end versions: sterling silver bands engraved with "WWJD," gold-plated necklaces, crystal paperweights. Soon there wasn't a surface that one couldn't imagine bearing the inscription "WWJD." There were bumper stickers, T-shirts, business cards, leather key chains, notecards…all asking the now-familiar question, "What Would Jesus Do?"

Well, he sure-as-shootin' wouldn't have spent his money on a WWJD T-shirt or key chain, but that's beside the point!

Actually, the concept was a good one. Presumably, anyone who sported the initials in some form or another took a moment on at least one occasion to ask the question, "What would Jesus do in this situation?" Not a bad question to use as a barometer for our actions.

As we've implied many times in this book though, true discipleship does not start with *actions* as much as *attitudes*. Too many discipleship programs get hung up because they concentrate so heavily on doing, that is, taking action as opposed to being. As we approach this next signpost, we'll see how a disciple's life will not mimic Christ's unless that life is infused with Scripture.

It wasn't too long into the bracelet craze before it became clear that a slogan does not a disciple make! You only have to be cut off in traffic by a car with a WWJD bumper sticker or treated rudely by someone wearing a WWJD bracelet to understand that there is a giant lapse between asking the question and living the answer.

A friend of mine (Rich), while working with a Christian publisher, launched a new campaign to close this gap. Although it doesn't fit on a bracelet very well, the new question is "HCYAWJWDIYDKWHD?" While I'm not going to buy stock in a new

QUEST EXPERIENCE

During the next thirty days, read through Romans 1–15 (you'll need to read a half chapter a day). Each day ask yourself these questions:

• What is one thing God has taught me through this passage?

• How does God want me to live out that truth today?

• Who does God want me to share that truth with?

• How will this truth transform me?

• How could this truth transform those I'm discipling?

line of bracelets with this impossibly long string of initials, the idea is a good one. The question here is "How Can You Ask What Jesus Would Do If You Don't Know What He Did?"

I might change the question to read, "How can you ask what Jesus would do if you don't know who he really *was?*" There's a connection

QUESTions

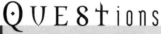

• Where have you learned the most about Jesus—from sermons, friends, a pastor, the Bible, or books?

• Ask several young adults where they've learned the most about Jesus. Any surprises?

between being and doing. You can't ask what Jesus would *do* until you understand who he *was*. By the same token, we won't consistently do the things of God until we become the people of God. As disciples, our actions won't mimic Christ's until our hearts do.

What about Jesus made him act the way he did? The sincerest bracelet wearer can't do what Jesus would do without first thinking about (and modeling) who Jesus is. The writer of Proverbs noted, "As a man thinks in his heart, so is he." The way we act is preceded by the way we think. I believe the Bible emphasizes belief, or being, before doing.

Let me say a word here so as not to be totally misunderstood. We're not saying you can't do the work of ministry before you know it all, just that you need to be

> **We won't consistently do the things of God until we become the people of God. As disciples, our actions won't mimic Christ's until our hearts do.**

in relationship as the primary place of beginning. Obviously, both are important. Compare Paul's views to James':

For it is by grace you have been saved, through faith—and this not from yourselves, it is the gift of God—not by works, so that no one can boast (Ephesians 2:8-9).

QUESTions

Go back and read assumption 4 in chapter 1: "The Quest." Then answer the following questions.

- What's the goal in Bible study?
  Consider what you want young adults to gain from studying the Bible.
- What kind of Bible study will best accomplish that?

What good is it, my brothers, if a man claims to have faith but has no deeds? Can such faith save him?...In the same way, faith by itself, if it is not accompanied by action, is dead.

But someone will say, "You have faith; I have deeds."

Show me your faith without deeds, and I will show you my faith by what I do (James 2:14, 17-18).

Paul tells us there is nothing we can do without God's grace. The very faith required to believe in God is supplied by God and not a result of our own efforts. James, on the other hand, reminds us that that faith must result in actions. We've got to be the people of God, and then we have to do the things of God.

GUIDED BY SCRIPTURE

The place we learn who Jesus was—and the instruction manual for who we are to be as the people of God—is God's Word. "All Scripture is inspired by God and profitable for teaching, for reproof, for correction, for training in righteousness" (2 Timothy 3:16, NASB). It's the encouragement for Christian faith and practice.

> " The Bible was never meant to be just a book of doctrines, but a book of stories of real-life people and their encounters with God. By recording their struggles, the Bible encourages us to live in a committed relationship with God. We strive to follow their example where appropriate and to follow God's commands where so directed. "

The Bible was never meant to be just a book of doctrines, but a book of stories of real-life people and their encounters with God. By recording their struggles, the Bible encourages us to live in a committed relationship with God. We strive to follow their example where appropriate and to follow God's commands where so directed.

The Bible is God's method book. Since the Bible is the basis for Christian practice, it serves as the guide for our methods of ministry (2 Corinthians 1:12). In the same way, the Bible helps us distinguish between absolutes and non-absolutes. Absolutes are biblical principles that do not vary with time or culture. Non-absolutes are the specific applications, which may vary with time or culture.

QUESTions

- What are your favorite stories from the Bible?

- What does it mean that "the Bible is not just a book of doctrines"?

- What does it mean that the Bible is "God's method book"?

For example, the Bible says, "Christians should gather together" (Hebrews 10:24-25); it does not say, "Christians should gather together on Sunday mornings, dress in suits, and sit in pews." As a matter of fact, many young adult ministries don't meet at all on Sunday mornings. Frontline meets on Sunday night. More than once someone has said, "How can you worship on Sunday nights? Don't you know that Sunday morning is when we're supposed to worship?" To which we say, we believe worship happens every day, but we gather weekly on Sunday night. The absolutes are eternal and unchanging, but we should have great freedom to change the non-absolutes, depending on the need of a particular situation.

At one point Dietrich Bonhoeffer, the German theologian and martyr, whom many today consider to be a model for discipleship, discovered he

was very involved in Christian work and yet without Christ at the center of his activities. His life was totally transformed by his dis- covery of the Bible. He had preached hun-

QUEStions

- How are Christians to be guided by Scripture?

- How can you encourage young adults to be guided by Scripture?

dreds of sermons, earned a doctorate in theology, taught Bible courses, and yet he had never become a Christian. He had even turned his faith

QUESt

EXPERIENCE

If you don't already have one, choose a life verse. Share that verse and its importance to you with your fellow travelers.

Ask several young adults about their life verse and tell them about yours. Encourage them to choose one if they don't already have one.

into something he could use for his own advantage, but apparently it had not changed him. But when he discovered the Bible, it changed him. He became com- mitted to being a servant of Jesus Christ and being a part of the church. When he discovered the Bible, he became the friend of God.[1]

Jesus explained how this works in John 15:15: "I no longer call you servants, because a servant does not know his mas- ter's business. Instead, I have called you friends, for everything that I learned from my Father I have made known to you."

Gordon McDonald tells a story of an old book that looked as if it had been often read, but when he opened the book, the pages were still stuck together; it was clear the book had never been read. Used, yes, but read, no. He concludes, "The Christian who is not growing intellectually is like a book whose many pages remain unopened and unread. Like the book, he may be of some value, but not nearly as much as if he had chosen to sharpen and develop his mind."[2]

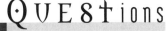

- The Bible changed Bonhoeffer. How is it changing you?

- How is it changing the young adults in your church?

Darrell Jodock talks about infusing the Scriptures into every cell in our bodies.[3] He points to Ezekiel 3, in which Ezekiel was handed a written scroll and told, "Eat what is before you, eat this scroll; then go and speak to the house of Israel" (Ezekiel 3:1). This is the kind of commitment to Scripture that will guide disciples on their quest for Christ.

We need to help young adults go back to the basics of their faith, to the place of *being* rather than *doing*. I must confess this is the place where I have to work the hardest. It's so easy to be a doer; being is hard work.

The other night my daughter Jessa called me into her room and said, "Dad, will you lie down with me and listen to my Bible reading?" Well, I was honored to be asked. As she finished reading, she recited a memory verse, then looked at me, and casually remarked, "Dad, Mom knows more Bible verses than you do." Suddenly her expression turned to horror as she realized what she had said to me. After all, I am the pastor; I am the paid Bible guy of the family!

Sitting with Jessa, I was tempted to feel horrible about my memory skills. After all, here I am advocating we be students of God's Word so we can become imitators of Christ. And then it hit me. Bible memorization isn't the measure of Christlikeness; it's just one more activity.

Is it a worthy activity? Sure. Do I wish I could memorize Scripture better? You bet. But the point of studying Scripture is not to add to my tally of memory verses; it's so I will become so steeped in God's Word that I live and breathe the life it represents. In my case, this will have to happen without a quiver full of memory verses. Memory skills or not, we've got to focus on the basics.

A year ago I was on the stationary bike in the weight room of a hotel where we were holding a young adult convention. A friend walked in and observed, "You look like you're going to die." I'd been on the stationary bike for only three minutes, but those three minutes seemed like forever.

During the last few years I had been so busy with work pursuits, I'd neglected the basics of physical health. My body had gone to pot. At 5 feet, 10 inches and nearly 210 pounds, I was walking death with a belly. I not only looked terrible, I felt terrible. For years I'd been working two and three projects at

·QUE8†ions

- How are you focusing on the basics with young adult disciples in your church? Are there other ways to do it?

Brainstorm at least twenty-five new ways to help young adults encounter Scripture in meaningful ways.

once to make ends meet, striving all the while to be a decent husband and father. I just never took the time to exercise. And so there I was trying to ride a bike for three minutes and nearly dying.

I'm trying to change that and am getting in better shape. Even though I've been working out on and off for several years, I still find it difficult. I hated working out on the day I started and I still do, but the struggle is necessary to be healthy. That's one of the basics for a healthy life. We need to show young adults what the

·QUE8†ions

- What are the basics of faith?

- In real, specific ways, how can you help young adults become fluent in the basics of faith?

basics are and, in the case of faith, the Bible is one of the basics. Fortunately, reading and studying it aren't nearly as difficult as working out!

The temptation for many here will be to say, "Wait a minute, this new world doesn't believe the Bible is authoritative, so why use it as the basis?" This is the same situation that Dietrich Bonhoeffer observed in Germany in the thirties when he referred to the world as "come of age."[4] It had become exactly the kind of world that the enlightenment, with its emphasis on scientific method, had destined it to become.

"Since Kant," Bonhoeffer observed, "he [God] has been relegated to a realm beyond the world of experience."[5] But, Bonhoeffer argued, his (and our) secularized society only served to whet the appetite for the things of God. He felt that the world that has come of age is more godless and, perhaps for that reason, nearer to God than the world before its coming of age.

The Bible is crucial because the Bible is God's message to us about how to really live. The Bible helps me to understand my world, my life, my crazy behavior, my guilt, my hope. It gives the answers I need for life, tells me who God is, and, finally, tells me how to love God. The reason the Bible is so important to me is that I have a relationship with the author of the Bible. His words are never trivial but always point toward some purpose.

How do we show postmodern young adults that God speaks to them through the Bible? We ask questions as we read together: What does this passage tell me about God? Who is the main character of the story, and what would his or her life have been like? What were his or her needs? What does the Bible tell me about the people of its pages? What is God telling me about me? What is he trying to show me about life and relationships? What is God asking me to do with this newfound information?

QUESTions

- In your setting, how would you answer the question, "How do we show postmodern young adults that God speaks to them through the Bible?"

By sitting together, in relationship, and showing that the Bible is all about relationships, we can erase the postmodern skeptic's sense that the Bible has become irrelevant.

NOTES

1. Eberhard Bethge, *Dietrich Bonhoeffer* (Minneapolis: Fortress Press, 2000), 205.
2. Gordon MacDonald, *Ordering Your Private World* (Nashville, TN: Oliver-Nelson, 1984), 110.
3. Darrell Jodock, *The Church's Bible: Its Contemporary Authority* (Minneapolis: Fortress Press, 1989), 143.
4. Dietrich Bonhoeffer, *Letters and Papers From Prison* (New York: Touchstone, 1997), 341.
5. Bonhoeffer, *Letters and Papers From Prison*, 341.

Signpost Seven

PROCESS

" Whatever a person is like, I try to find a common ground with him so that he will let me tell him about Christ and let Christ save him. "

—1 Corinthians 9:22b, *The Living Bible*

" The Church, in the Western world, faces populations who are increasingly 'secular'—people with no Christian memory... These populations are increasingly 'postmodern'; they have graduated from Enlightenment ideology and are more peer driven, feeling driven, and 'right-brained' than their forebears. "

—George G. Hunter III, *The Celtic Way of Evangelism*

Two years ago my wife Susan and I (Ken) joined our local Gold's Gym. We're working on getting into better shape, as Rich is. We were excited about spending time together working out each day and have become very dedicated, often spending an hour and a half in the gym each day except Sunday.

Over the course of time, we've gotten to know many "gym rats" and have had many great conversations with them about Christ. I became particularly close with a competing bodybuilder named Brian. When he found out that I was a pastor (which he found interesting, due to the fact that I was so intense in my workouts), he was not dissuaded, but our conversations never centered on Christ.

Yet one day, after I'd known Brian for over a year, he surprised me. Brian was spotting me on the incline bench and right in the middle of my set with heavy dumbbells in each hand while going for my last rep, he blurts out, "Ken, how do you know that Christianity is the right way to God?" I almost dropped the weights on my face. Needless to say, that opened the door for some great conversation.

QUEStions

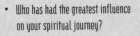

- Who has had the greatest influence on your spiritual journey?

- How did they help you come to Christ?

Here's what I learned with Brian: People that you build a friendship with will eventually come around to asking you about Christ. When you allow the Spirit of God to work in people through prayer and time, you'll find that God prepares their hearts to be receptive to the gospel. Then when the opportune time presents itself (usually by them asking a question), you have the privilege of sharing the story of Christ with them.

Another important issue to understand is the basic skepticism that many young adults have toward Christianity. Their skepticism is merited

QUEStions

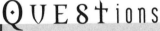

- Why do you think people are skeptical about Christianity?

- How can you tailor your evangelism efforts to answer their skepticism?

in that they have seen so much scandal in the church, such as news reports of the clergy abusing their positions of power.

People today take time to watch your life to see if you live by what you profess to believe. Once they find out you're a Christian, they watch you, perhaps for a long time, and then when they feel that you have credibility, they'll ask a question that opens the door to sharing Christ. Evangelism with today's postmodern young adults is largely based on your credibility, and the only way to demonstrate credibility is over time.

As a result of his research with a variety of individuals, George G. Hunter notes the importance of credibility when sharing the gospel message. He says, "My interview research with secular people has confirmed the prominence of the 'credibility' theme in secular people's inquires about Christianity, and their inquiries often take one of three specific forms. First, some people wonder whether we really believe what we say we believe. Second, some people do not doubt that we believe it; they wonder whether we live by it. Third, some people do not doubt that we believe it or live by it; they wonder whether it makes much difference!"[1]

> " Evangelism with today's postmodern young adults is largely based on your credibility, and the only way to demonstrate credibility is over time. "

Credibility takes time, especially with this generation. For that reason we've labeled our next signpost "Process." Journeying on the quest for Christ with a young adult in today's generation, you'll have to cultivate an attitude of process and patience. Throw out your previous ideas about the chronology of one's faith development. Put away any idea of A, then B, then C—meaning evangelism, followed by faith commitment, followed by discipleship. This may not be an accurate model for today's young adults.

QUE8tions

- Do you have credibility with non-Christians?

- How is credibility established?

The more likely scenario is that these events will often overlap as the young adult moves through disinterest to skepticism to reluctant belief to sold-out servanthood, often taking one step back for every two steps forward. To be sure, the event of commitment to and confession of Christ is no less important than it's always been, but how we get them there is what the process is all about. This non-sequential route to Christ formation is called process evangelism.

"Process evangelism? What's that? you ask. I've heard of street evangelism, where I confront strangers about their sinful condition, separation from God, and need of a Savior.

"I've heard of friendship evangelism, where I build a relationship with a co-worker, fellow student, or workout partner with the ultimate goal of winning them to the faith.

"I've heard of lifestyle evangelism, where I move in stealth mode among my peers and co-workers, hoping that my attitudes and actions will elicit an inquiry as to why I'm different.

"I've even heard of servant evangelism, where I volunteer in different places to serve others with a no-strings-attached attitude in hopes that my altruism will be noticed and will spawn a conversation which will provide an opportunity for me to share my God story.

"But what is this process evangelism? Please tell me that this is not some new means of watering down the gospel to such an extent that we neglect to confront people about their sin and need of a Savior."

Rest assured, process evangelism is not a watered-down version of the gospel that tries to make it more palatable for secular people. Instead, process evangelism is a type of evangelistic paradigm that provides a more effective way of looking at evangelism in a postmodern culture.

In 1 Corinthians 3:5-9 we find the Apostle Paul himself using organic metaphors to describe the process of evangelism. He says, "Who do you

QUES†ions

- What is your definition of evangelism?

- Have you lived that out? Why or why not?

think Paul is, anyway? Or Apollos, for that matter? Servants, both of us—servants who waited on you as you gradually learned to entrust your lives to our mutual Master. We each carried out our servant assignment. I planted the seed, Apollos watered the plants, but *God* made you grow. It's not the one who plants or the one who waters who is at the center of this process but God, who makes things grow. Planting and watering are menial servant jobs at minimum wages. What makes them worth doing is the God we are serving. You happen to be God's field in which we are working" *(The Message).*

Notice three things from this passage. First, Paul notes that a person's

QUEST

EXPERIENCE

Buy an African violet for yourself and each of your fellow travelers. Care for the plant for several weeks. Each time you're together with your fellow travelers, discuss how the violet is doing.

- Is your violet thriving or dying under your care? Why?

- How is tending the violets a metaphor for evangelism? for discipleship?

coming to Christ is a process; it's something the Corinthians *"gradually learned."*

Second, every Christian plays a vital, yet distinct role in a secular person's coming to Christ based on his or her giftedness. Paul says that he was the one who planted the seed. The seed, of course, is the Word of God. In Matthew 13:1-9, 18-23, Jesus likens the human heart to soil and the Word of God to seed. Some of us sow the seed, our job is to just scatter the seed everywhere we go. Apollos, on the other hand, watered the new plants giving them nourishment, while it was God who brought the growth. Paul described a person's coming to Christ as a process in which God is the master gardener, and we are his workers. "One laborer plows the soil, another sows the seed, a third waters the seed. As time passes, the plants grow, the fruit appears, and other laborers enjoy reaping the harvest."[2]

Third, it's critical to note that all the effort that we put into sowing seed, planting, and watering are nothing unless God makes it grow. This brings us to God's sovereignty.

QUESTIONS

- What do you think your role is in bringing others to Christ?

- How do you think the young adults in your church are gifted in evangelism?

Understanding the sovereignty of God in the evangelism process is extremely important. It means that I can relax and share my faith without compulsion or manipulation. I don't have to use emotional ploys or fear tactics. My part in a person's spiritual journey (determined by my spiritual giftedness) may simply be to plant the seed and nothing more. I may or may not have the privilege of seeing that seed grow into spiritual commitment.

Each of us needs to be faithful to our part in bringing a person to Christ, leaving the result up to God. The reason I'm being so emphatic here is because I see too many people forcing God down other's throats. I'm sure their intentions are pure; they have a genuine concern for the eternal well-being of the person they're sharing with. But they neutralize the process of evangelism when they're driven to plant, water, and harvest in a ten-minute presentation of the gospel. People sometimes do make professions for Christ in such circumstances. But usually when people genuinely respond to such a presentation, they're already ripe for harvest. They have heard the gospel before.

> " Understanding the sovereignty of God in the evangelism process is extremely important. It means that I can relax and share my faith without compulsion or manipulation. "

QUE8tions

- Have you ever "forced" the gospel on someone or discussed Christ with someone who has had the gospel forced on them?

- What did you learn from that experience? Did it change the way you share Christ?

So relax when sharing your faith. Don't force things. Plant the seeds or pour on a little water. Don't try and call a person to commitment too soon. Just as a seed may take weeks to sprout and break through the surface of the ground, a person making a commitment to Christ needs time.

> " So relax when sharing your faith. Don't force things. Plant the seeds or pour on a little water. Don't try and call a person to commitment too soon. Just as a seed may take weeks to sprout and break through the surface of the ground, a person making a commitment to Christ needs time. "

Process evangelism allows a person to gradually come to understand the claims of Christ and make an informed decision. You can't force this process; all you can do is your part (sowing, planting, watering, or harvesting) and trust God to grow the seed and bring it to fruition.

So how does all this process evangelism work? It allows for all the other evangelic tools we have already noted to be used in their proper context (street evangelism, friendship evangelism, lifestyle evangelism, and servant evangelism). As the old saying goes, "If all you have is a hammer, every-thing looks like a nail." Process evangelism is not a tool in and of itself; think of it instead as the various stages a secular person goes through while on their journey toward Christ. Let's take a look at what these various stages look like.

THE STAGES OF PROCESS EVANGELISM

Stage 1: Realization

Process evangelism begins when we as evangelists realize a lost person's spir-itual condition and, as a result, respond with hearts full of compassion—this is where all evangelism must begin. The Bible is clear that people without Christ are spiritually dead and separated from God. What compounds this realization is our understanding of the spiritual battle that is raging for their souls. We know that Satan's goal is to blind the eyes of non-Christians so they don't see their true condition and their desperate need for a Savior.

QUEStions

- Do you have compassion for those who don't know Christ?

- Do the young adults you disciple have this compassion?

- How can you cultivate true compassion and love toward non-Christians?

A non-Christian is simply Satan's prey. Satan's the hunter. He's the lion looking for someone to devour, the serial killer planning his next attack, the evil stranger seducing the little girl into his car with sweet talk and candy, only to victimize her and leave her body in a Dumpster down some dark alley. Satan is evil and deceptive; let's not downplay that reality. And non-Christians are totally unaware of his presence and his tactics.

This realization should compel us to compassionately intervene in what-ever way we can to show non-Christians the truth of their situation and God's amazing solution. It's not unlike seeing a car out of control, careen-ing down the street toward a little child in a crosswalk, unaware of her impending fate. What would you do? Of course, your heart would beat with concern, compassion for her situation would run through your veins like adrenaline, and you'd risk your own life to push her out of the way.

The same is true when we come to realize the situation and fate of non-Christians. We know they're unaware of the spiritual battle raging around them. We know that Satan has blinded their eyes to the truth of their condition and the claims of Christ. We know the result if they never hear the gospel and respond— eternal separation from God in hell. So instead of looking at non-Christians with contempt or frustration because of their lack of responsiveness to our evangelistic efforts, we must first reach out to them with compassion and sincere concern.

> " Process evangelism is not a tool in and of itself; think of it instead as the various stages a secular person goes through while on their journey toward Christ. "

Stage 2: Recognition

At this stage we must recognize that each non-Christian is a unique image bearer of God and dearly loved. As such, each person is valuable to God and worthy of a significant investment of our time.

Through the parables of the lost sheep, the lost coin, and the lost son, Luke 15 reminds us of the heart of God toward those who are lost. In each parable we see God's willingness to search, his patience to wait, and his rejoicing when the lost are found.

By its nature, process evangelism takes time and patience as we wait for people to gradually learn and embrace the truths of Christ. Each person is highly valued by God, and we must patiently invest our time and our energy rather than rushing people to some decision point before they're ready. People are not robots that we can command to operate according to our timetable and agenda.

> " By its nature, process evangelism takes time and patience as we wait for people to gradually learn and embrace the truths of Christ... People are not robots that we can command to operate according to our timetable and agenda. "

This stage also recognizes that God's in control of the growth process and that our job is to play our unique role according to where people are and what our giftedness is. God loves people, and God must call them in order for them to respond. God only needs us to plant, water, and harvest—all of which take time.

James Engel and William Dyrness note the importance of patience in the process of evangelism. "An attempt to motivate this response prematurely can quickly bring about misunderstanding, resentment and even a short-lived, insincere faith."[3] Patience is a fruit of the Spirit; allow that fruit to manifest itself in your evangelistic efforts.

> **" Patience is a fruit of the Spirit; allow that fruit to manifest itself in your evangelistic efforts. "**

Stage 3: Acceptance

Acceptance can be a very confusing term for people. Some think that to accept someone means that you condone sinful behavior, while others see acceptance as something you give to someone after the behavior has already changed. Paul clears up the confusion. He says, "Accept one another, then, just as Christ accepted you" (Romans 15:7a).

Henry Cloud and John Townsend define acceptance as "the state of receiving someone into relationship. To be accepted is to have all of your parts, good and bad, received by another without condemnation."[4]

It's possible to accept a person without condoning sinful behavior. Jesus modeled this with the woman at the well (John 4:4-26). His acceptance of her is evident simply in the fact that he stopped and talked to her. In the first century for a man, especially a man of Jesus' reputation as a rabbi, to talk to a woman alone, and a Samaritan woman at that, is ample evidence of his acceptance of her. But Jesus didn't let her off the hook in regard to her sinful behavior. Jesus confronted her about having had many husbands and also about living with a man who was not her husband. Jesus accepted her, but he also directed her to stop her life of sin.

At this stage we meet people where they are instead of where we think they should be or even where we would like them to be. My friend Brian introduced me to his girlfriend, whom he lives with certain days of each week depending on their hectic schedules. Of course, I don't condone their living together, but neither have I confronted him about this. There will come a time for that.

Brian does not share my biblical value system, and I can't expect him to. How can I expect him to live as a Christian before he becomes one? Yet, by accepting him where he is, we will build a relationship over time, which I believe will influence him to make a commitment to Christ. With Jesus in his life, his value system will begin to change and then so will his behavior.

Dallas Willard agrees. He says, "We frankly need to do much less of this managing of action, and especially with young people. We need to concentrate on changing the minds of those we would reach and serve. What they do will certainly follow, as Jesus well understood and taught."[5]

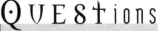

QUESTions

• Are you accepting of non-Christians? Is your church?

• Practically, how do you accept people and show them love without condoning their behavior?

Acceptance is a very important part of process evangelism that we must embrace if we're to reach today's postmodern young adults for Christ. This is especially true where we live in the Washington, D.C. area.

In Washington, D.C. we're never lacking for people who want our church to take up various causes. Whether the cause is homosexuality, abortion, or a certain political agenda, people want our church to champion their cause. Yet we do not. It's not that we don't have a biblical standpoint on all these issues; we do. However, we're not an issue-centered church; we're a Christ-centered church.

Can you imagine if we had a pro-life Sunday and turned over the pulpit to another organization that was unfamiliar with our culture here in Washington? They wouldn't know the sensibilities and means by which to communicate the pro-life truths of God's Word to our culture. Can you see the damage that could be done to our ability to be a place for a woman who has had an abortion to accept Christ?

We don't take a public stand on a host of issues because issues are not the issue—Christ is the issue. Bringing people to Jesus Christ will give them the ability to internalize the values and ways of Christ over time. We focus on accepting people where they are, but loving them too much to leave them there.

Recently I was doing a series at Frontline on sex, and one of the issues I dealt with was sex before marriage. I talked about why that was not God's best and what the Bible says about it, namely that it's sin.

I received an e-mail from a first-time visitor that night (my e-mail address is published in our weekly bulletin, and yes, I get a ton of e-mail!) who was very upset with me. She told me that she and her boyfriend were living together and that neither of them were Christians. She said they were hoping that our church would be a place where they could experience God without being condemned.

Well, I was sorry that they felt condemned, and I was certainly careful in what I said from the pulpit so that I wouldn't offend unnecessarily, but I'm also very aware that the gospel message is offensive and foolish to non-Christians. I'm not going to change my message. I feel that God used me in that situation to scatter

> "We don't take a public stand on a host of issues because issues are not the issue—Christ is the issue."

some seed. Though it might be a long time until that seed takes root, I believe that God will use it in their lives and that God's Word will not come back void. Being accepting of people is never an excuse to condone sinful behavior. As we engage secular people in dialogue, and they find out we're Christians, we need to be very careful not to come across as condemning.

It's amazing to me how many times I strike up a conversation with someone, and it eventually comes around to the dreaded question, "What do you do for a living?" I often cringe, not because I'm ashamed of my vocation as a pastor; I cringe because of the typical response I get. People either don't believe me because they don't think I look the part (a pastor wearing a black leather jacket and driving a Mustang convertible is a disconnect with some people). Or they react with the statement, "Oh, that must be very rewarding," unable to hide the condescending tone in their

> "For some reason, people have the idea that a Christian is a judgmental, self-righteous, intolerant, and mean-spirited person. Let's think for a moment. Is that how Jesus was perceived? Certainly not!"

voice. Or worse, they assume that they have said something wrong, and I will judge them or look down on them. It seems as if non-Christians have a host of assumptions about those of us with the titles of minister or Christian. But how in the world did they ever come up with these ideas?

In his book *What's So Amazing About Grace?* Phillip Yancey gives us insight into this question by telling the story of a friend who works with the down-and-out in the inner city of Chicago.

> A prostitute came to me [Yancey's friend said] in wretched straits, homeless, sick, and unable to buy food for her two-year-old daughter. Through sobs and tears, she told me she had been renting out her daughter—two years old!—to men interested in kinky sex. She made more renting out her daughter for an hour than she could earn on her own in a night. She had to do it, she said, to support her own drug habit...At last I asked if she had ever thought of going to a church for help. I will never forget the look of pure, naive shock that crossed her face. "Church!" she cried. "Why would I ever go there? I was already feeling terrible about myself. They'd just make me feel worse."[6]

For some reason, people have the idea that a Christian is a judgmental, self-righteous, intolerant, and mean-spirited person. Let's think for a moment—Is that how Jesus was perceived? Certainly not! In fact, Jesus was verbally attacked more by the religious leaders of his day than by any sinner he encountered. Religious leaders accused Jesus of being a party animal. "The Son of Man came eating and drinking, and they say, 'He is a glutton and a drunkard, a friend of tax collectors and "sinners" ' " (Matthew 11:19).

QUEStions

- What has led to the perception that Christians are judgmental, self-righteous, intolerant, and mean-spirited?

- How does that affect evangelism?

- How can you change that perception among young adults?

Jesus said of himself: "For God did not send his Son into the world to condemn the world, but to save the world through him" (John 3:17).

Jesus was able to accept sinners in spite of their sin, yet he never condoned sin, nor should we. Acceptance is a key stage in process evangelism.

Stage 4: Graciousness

I've seen far too many examples of people sharing their faith and, instead of creating a dialogue, they cause an argument. They seem angry and hostile, and they put secular listeners on the defensive. Non-Christians are quick to protect themselves from a barrage of evidence that they are sinners on the road to hell.

Peter tells us to "always be prepared to give an answer to everyone who asks you to give the reason for the hope that you have. But do this with *gentleness and respect"* (1 Peter 3:15, italics added).

> *The intensity with which many share the gospel is neither biblical nor appropriate and often does more harm than good.*

Our attitude toward secular people must be gracious! We must be gentle and respectful, not harsh, abusive, or condemning. The intensity with which many share the gospel is neither biblical nor appropriate and often does more harm than good. Paul tells us, "Let your conversation be always *full of grace,* seasoned with salt, so that you may know how to answer everyone" (Colossians 4:6, italics added).

It's interesting to note that Jesus never shouted down a non-Christian. Instead, his harshest actions such as turning over the money-changers' tables in the Temple, and his harshest words, "You snakes! You brood of vipers!" were reserved for the religious leaders of his day (see Matthew 23:13-33). To be most effective in light of today's hostility toward Christianity, which is due in part to the often accurate perception that we're hypocrites, we need to be gracious as we talk with skeptical non-Christians.

Stage 5: Competence

At this stage, we're now ready to talk about how to use the various evangelistic tools we noted in the beginning of this chapter. Each of the tools has a unique role in sharing the gospel, but which one you use depends largely on the environment you're in. Some situations will require a more relational approach in which lifestyle, friendship, or service evangelism is most appropriate. Other situations lend themselves to a more direct approach such as street evangelism. At Frontline we practice service evangelism almost exclusively.

The basic premise of service evangelism is quite simple. You go into your community and serve people by handing out cold drinks, washing windows, or raking leaves. When people in the community ask about your project, you simply respond that you're sharing God's love.

We've found that when you serve someone humbly rather than confronting them with some truth, you get a much different response. Instead of putting the person on the defensive, they ask you questions like, "Why are you doing this?" or "What's in this for you?"

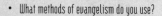

QUESTions

- What methods of evangelism do you use?
- Are young adults involved in evangelism?
- What steps could you take to involve more young adults in evangelism?

A few years ago a blizzard hit the East coast. I measured forty-six inches of snow outside my house. Needless to say, the storm shut down the entire city of Washington, D.C. and surrounding areas. Lon Solomon, the senior pastor of McLean Bible Church, called me and suggested we mobilize a bunch of Frontliners to go and shovel snow out of people's driveways. Wishing I had thought up the idea, I enthusiastically called a bunch of guys and deployed them in SUVs to the area surrounding our church.

As they were shoveling snow, a news truck pulled up to one of the teams and asked the team what it was doing.

David, who was a key volunteer leader, responded, "We're a bunch of young adults from the church down the road, and we wanted to come out and help people." When the reporter asked if they were being paid, David said, "No, we're just sharing the love of God in a practical way." Smelling a good story, the reporters turned on their cameras, and David found himself on the evening news totally uncensored, telling

QUESTions

- How do you think David's experience affected his own personal quest for Christ?
- What role does evangelizing play in discipleship?
- How could evangelizing affect the faith journeys of the young adults in your church?

everyone that by shoveling driveways for free they were sharing the love of God they experienced through a relationship with Jesus Christ. David had an amazing opportunity to share the gospel with the entire Washington, D.C. area.

The important thing to remember when considering the stages of process evangelism is that it's not a systematic approach to sharing the gospel. Instead, it's a paradigm for sharing the gospel in a postmodern culture. When think-ing through the var-ious ways that Jesus shared with people, you won't find a preconceived tactic that he used in every situation.

QUE8ᴛions

- Are you sensitive to the process of evangelism?

- What steps can you take to nurture the process of evangelism from soil preparation all the way to final harvest?

Consider the different responses Jesus gave to Nicodemus (John 3:3) and the woman at the well (John 4:10), or Zacchaeus (Luke 19:9) and the woman who led a sinful life (Luke 7:50), or the rich young ruler (Matthew 19:21) and the woman caught in adultery (John 8:11).

"Jesus adapted his strategy to each unique situation, while always remaining true to the biblical pattern of God's dealings with Israel and the world."[7] Likewise, in order for the church to be effective in reaching young postmoderns for Christ, we need to be much more sensitive to the process of evangelism instead of soliciting an oftentimes forced response.

NOTES

1. George G. Hunter III, *The Celtic Way of Evangelism: How Christianity Can Win the West...Again* (Nashville, TN: Abingdon Press, 2000), 60.
2. Warren W. Wiersbe, *The Bible Exposition Commentary, Vol. 1* (Wheaton, IL: Victor Books, 1989), 579.
3. James F. Engel and William A. Dyrness, *Changing the Mind of Missions* (Downers Grove, IL: InterVarsity Press, 2000), 101.
4. Henry Cloud and John Townsend, *How People Grow* (Grand Rapids, MI: Zondervan Publishing House, 2001), 149.
5. Dallas Willard, *The Divine Conspiracy: Rediscovering Our Hidden Life With God* (San Francisco: Harper San Francisco, 1998), 307.
6. Phillip Yancey, *What's So Amazing About Grace?* (Grand Rapids, MI: Zondervan Publishing House, 1997), 11.
7. Engle and Dyrness, *Changing the Mind of Missions,* 106.

Signpost Eight _____

PERSONHOOD

" *Let us make man
in our image.* "

–Genesis 1:26

" *We strive continually to adorn
and preserve our imaginary self,
neglecting the true one.* "

–Blaise Pascall

The final signpost we'll discuss is "Personhood," the understanding that each person has value for the simple reason that he or she bears the image of God. To successfully guide another on the quest for Christ, one must understand the importance of personhood.

One of my (Rich's) favorite young adult congregations, which meets in Denver, understands this very well. The congregation is co-pastored by Mike and Reese. Reese fits the demographic of the church membership; Mike is twenty years older than most of the congregation. Mike and Reese value the personhood of the members and visitors to their church, and therefore self-expression is an important ethic in their thinking. Mike and Reese do everything they can to disciple the congregation with a very loose hold.

When the church was new and needed a name, the members—who tend to be pierced and tattooed—named themselves Scum of the Earth, after 1 Corinthians 4:11-13: "To this very hour we go hungry and thirsty, we are in rags, we are brutally treated, we are homeless. We work hard with our own hands. When we are cursed, we bless; when we are persecuted, we endure it; when we are slandered, we answer kindly. Up to this moment we have become the scum of the earth, the refuse of the world."

They have expressed themselves in other ways that seem right to them. When some suggested they wear clothing with the name of the church, they chose black knit hats. The church newsletter, called the 'zine, has enough typefaces, sketches, and stream-of-consciousness copy to make a concrete sequential person wince. The worship team, on the other hand, is led by a young woman named Deva and has a folk-rock feel one might hear at the Lillith Fair—even though the ska-core band, Five Iron Frenzy, is at the core of the leadership team. Keeping self-expression a high value, the church has produced two ten-minute films about itself that most postmoderns find hilarious but that regularly offend an older crowd.

Small groups are not formed around convenient locations in the city or which book of the Bible the group is studying, but rather around common interests. There's the girls skateboarding small group, the graphic artists small group, the modern culture small group, the people-who-are-trying-to-learn-Spanish small group, and others based on similar interests. These groups still study the Scriptures and are committed to serving the poor of the city, but they gather as friends who share unique perspectives on life.

Scum, as it's affectionately called, understands personhood. People who come to Scum of the Earth church know instantly that they matter and are valued for who they are, not what they might or might not do. To a generation that values being real over being normal, young adult churches like Scum of the Earth offer the kind of environment that encourages discipleship.

KNOWING THE TIMES

If we're going to develop disciples for a postmodern world, we need to better grasp and appreciate the impact of postmodernism. Whether you use the term postmodernism, post-Christian, or post-churched, anyone who wants to disciple a young adult today needs to understand the times as did the men of Issachar in 1 Chronicles 12:32 "who understood the times and knew what Israel should do." We believe the personhood signpost leads us to a better understanding of the times and will lead us to know what to do.

> " If we're going to develop disciples for a postmodern world, we need to better grasp and appreciate the impact of postmodernism. "

·QUE8tions

Describe how the young adults you know have felt marginalized by the church.

- What mistakes has the church made in the way it presents God and Christianity to young adults?

- How can you rectify this in your own discipling relationships?

We're living in a time when many young adults mistrust reason and, along with that, the Christian message that the Bible is truth. So how do you establish truth in a changing world that processes truth in a new way? All the systems we have used up to this point to explain our world and our beliefs are being abandoned by some because they do not trust knowledge. Everyone's understanding of life is considered as valid as the next person's; therefore my truth is mine, your truth is yours, and each is equally valid and has no tie to universal truth. You can imagine the way this belief is transforming every area of everyday life as it impacts law, health, education, media, and even people's quest for Christ!

The thinkers whose thoughts have influenced postmodern young adults are Michel Foucault, Jacques Derrida, and Pierre Bourdieu. What they have done in their writings is attempt to carry the ideas of modern thinking to their radical conclusions. They propose that knowledge is not a neutral tool for learning; in fact, knowledge is uncertain and should be abandoned. They claim that the world is not progressing, which the twentieth century has made plain with AIDS, hunger, and the failure of political

> " No longer do we live and learn in isolation but in community. Postmodern thinkers claim that truth is understood not by reason but by feeling and intuition. "

structures. No longer do we live and learn in isolation but in community. They claim that truth is understood not by reason but by feeling and intuition. Our world isn't shaped by powerful minds but by powerful forces like the Internet, not by intellects but by entertainers.

So, does the Bible have the ability to reach and shape a young adult who has been molded by thoughts like these? Yes! In fact, the very reason to tell young adults the gospel story is that it engages and empowers young adults with its emphasis on relationship. The biblical story teaches that humans are made in the image of God, and this is good news to young adults who are conditioned to think there's nothing about anything—themselves included—that is unique or special. But because we are made in the image of God, we have intrinsic worth because of who we are and not instrumental worth, which is based on what we do.

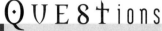

QUEStions

- Are postmodern thoughts contrary to a Christian worldview? Why or why not?

- How has postmodern thought affected discipleship?

Intrinsic value, once it's understood, is something that appeals to the postmodern mind. People are deemed important not by the seat they fill, the money they give, or the task they accomplish, but because they're created by God. Let me show you another way to look at this.

When evangelical churches use art, too often they emphasize the instrumental worth (the usefulness) of art. By art, we mean much more than music. We're speaking of drama, video, paintings, banners, photography, dance, and other artistic expressions. Instead of appreciating the creative endeavor as a representation of that part of our image bearing, we ask if the art has a practical application. Did it lead people to Christ? Is the Christian message explicit? Did the art support the sermon?

We separate art into two categories, Christian and secular. If it's Christian, then it has to lead someone to a relationship with Christ. If it's secular, it's to be avoided and surely not purchased or interpreted. When we lose art as a communication form with this generation, we lose the primary way of communicating to young adults.

QUESt EXPERIENCE

Find a picture of the paintings in the Sistine Chapel. With your fellow travelers, describe what you see.

- Why do the paintings have value?

- How is a person's worth measured by others?

- How is a person's worth measured by God?

Another factor which is a sign of the times is pluralism. Stanley Grentz talked about the importance of pluralism to postmoderns in his book *A Primer on Postmodernism*. He points out that the modern man has tended to look at people from a conquest mentality. When we see people as things to be conquered (in that we want them to know and do what we want), we are living out that conquest mentality. That mentality motivated the evangelism and discipleship efforts for earlier generations, but it has no appeal for this generation. To this generation, no one culture is superior to another. Every culture can learn from the others. Tolerance and respect are highly valued. These are the values and virtues esteemed by the new generations of young adults.

What the conquest mentality does is reduce the person to a number, a tick in the column of souls won, and not a bearer of the *imago dei*, the image of God. When the most important thing is to get a person to make some kind of decision and then get them into a pew (or in these days of church-growth strategies: a

·QUE8†ions

- In what ways does the church view young adults with a conquest mentality?

- How could you work to change that?

padded theatre-style seat), we find our efforts not reaping very much in the way of sold-out discipleship. While some churches swell in numbers, others shrink. We see a net gain of zero and seem to have very little ability to penetrate the culture we live in. Why?

The conquest mentality that flowed from the Enlightenment through colonialism, through the industrial age, and through Western expansion, made its way

> ❝ The conquest mentality that flowed from the Enlightenment through colonialism through the industrial age, and through Western expansion, made its way straight into our ideas about discipleship, bringing with it an emphasis on quantifiable results. ❞

straight into our ideas about discipleship, bringing with it an emphasis on quantifiable results. As a result, we emphasized the number of people we could bring in the door, the numbers we could sign up for our classes, and the numbers we could send out to gather the next batch of recruits. Lost in all of the "how-many," of course, was the "who." The person behind the numbers mattered less and less, until the current generation rose up to call us into account.

IMAGE BEARERS

When the emphasis is on the instrumental value of a pursuit, the bottom line lies somewhere other than in the practice per se. Worship becomes valuable only if it leads others to Christ or gives me a certain experience. Mercy is practiced only if it can be demonstrated to evangelize more people or bring church growth. This reduces one's relationship with God to a results-oriented relationship as opposed to a relationship full of imagination.

In contrast, Christian love sees the intrinsic value of the beloved. This is an important concept for young adults, many of whom have been raised in an environment where value is determined by productivity. As Loston Harris expressed in the introduction, many young adults feel they are judged by the what-have-you-done-for-me-lately crowd.

> "Postmodern young adults in our churches are sensitive to the tendency to judge things by their usefulness, and they are put off by it."

If I do not truly love you, I see you as one of the many objects in my world—something replaceable, like a ballplayer or an actor. Your value is your ability to perform certain functions, which others could also perform; therefore you're not indispensable. But the one thing no one else can ever do is to be you. I value that and see your indispensability only if I love you for your own sake, not for my sake or for your function's sake. If I do not love you, I see you as a mere object in the world; if I love you, I see you as the center of a world—

QUEStions

* Describe what the church would look like if it emphasized the intrinsic worth of young adults?

your world—as indispensable as I see myself.

The church today falls short of this ideal. Postmodern young adults in our churches are sensitive to the tendency to judge things by their usefulness, and they are put off by it. They suspect they might be judged by the same criterion. His or her "person" wants to be valued for their intrinsic worth, not for an ability to conform to another's expectations. Take my friend Wayne as an example.

Wayne is a great friend. We've spent great times together at church, at each other's homes, and on the ski slopes, where I ski while Wayne rides (snowboards). I really enjoy sharing ideas and dreams with him. He's one of the most creative people I know and a great friend to have. He's also a genius with video, and every pastor or speaker I know wants him to make videos for their talks.

Early on I decided I didn't care if he ever made a video for me; what I

> **The New Testament teaches us that the purpose of salvation is to have your 'God image' restored.**

cared about was Wayne. There are not many people I would rather hang out with, and there's hardly anyone else outside my family I like skiing with as much as Wayne. Had I looked at him for what he could do for me, I would have missed so much in terms of a relationship. Instead, I make time to listen to his spiritual frustrations and his journey, and he to mine.

Wayne and I are now doing ministry together and every time he sees me he smiles and so do I. I sometimes laugh when people get upset that they can't get him to do what they want, and I want to say, "You know what? Wayne would die for you, if he thought you cared about him and not just about what he can do for you."

What I'm doing is respecting Wayne's *imago dei*, the image of God in him. To respect a young adult's image is to love because God is love (1 John 4:7-8). Our purpose is to love, not to use. The New Testament teaches us that the purpose of salvation is to have your "God image" restored. Paul says, "Do not lie to each other, since you have taken off your old self with its practices and have put on the new self, which is being renewed in knowledge in the image of its Creator" (Colossians 3:9-10). What Paul is describing here is the process of sanctification.

As we help young adults to grow on their quest, we're helping them to be renewed in the image of God. We all who "reflect the Lord's glory are being transformed into his likeness" (2 Corinthians 3:18a). Our goal is to help young adults be like God: "Be imitators of God, as dearly loved children" (Ephesians 5:1).

FINDING IDENTITY IN CHRIST

The first step toward becoming an imitator of God is to understand who God is. To many young adults, figuring out what God is like is a profound and puzzling mystery that eludes solution.

When a police detective wants to find out who has committed a crime, he'll begin with what is already known. The *where, how,* and *why* of the crime will eventually lead to the *who.* In the same way, as we help young adults understand who they are in Christ, it's helpful to show them that God already has the where, how, and why of their lives under his control. Once they can see this,

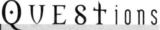

QUEStions

- How can you help young adults understand God better and thus understand themselves better?

- How will this help them in their quest for Christ?

they are more able to understand their true identity in him. Let me use the life of Abraham to explain this.

Where? "The Lord said to Abram, 'Leave your country, your people and your father's household and go to the land I will show you'" (Genesis 12:1). God asked Abraham to get up and move. The only thing is that God didn't tell him where he was moving to. He just said he was going to be moving. I can imagine Abraham had a lot of questions:

"Where am I going?"

The Lord said, "I'll let you know."

Abraham: "How long will it take?"

The Lord: "I'll let you know."

Abraham: "How do I know when I get there?"

The Lord: "I'll let you know."

Hebrews 11:8 says Abraham "obeyed and went, even though he did not know where he was going." He left immediately without excuse.

As we help young adults explore who they are in Christ, we can start by asking them to trust God for where he wants them to be. *Where should I work? Where should I live? Where should I retire? Where should I go to school?* Have them ask God for the answers to these questions and then act on faith that he'll lead them to where he wants them to be. Encourage them to hear God saying, as he did to Abraham, "You get moving first, and I will direct you."

> ❝ As we help young adults explore who they are in Christ, we can start by asking them to trust God for where he wants them to be. ❞

How? Perhaps Abraham was willing to trust God for the where of his life because he had been given the promise that he would become a great nation. Well, a great nation implies a lot of people, and at the time Abraham trusted God and left home, he and his wife had no children. To make matters more confusing, Abraham and Sarah were both elderly. Abraham must have wondered when God would make good on his promise. How could he become a great nation if he and his wife continued to be childless into their very old age?

In Genesis 18, we learn that God sent messengers to tell Abraham and his wife that what he had promised would be fulfilled and that this impossible situation was going to be turned into a miracle.

> "Where is your wife Sarah?" they asked Abraham. "There in the tent," he said. Then the Lord said, "I will surely return to you about this time next year, and Sarah your wife will have a son." Now Sarah was listening at the entrance of the tent, which was behind him. Abraham and Sarah were already old and well advanced in years, and Sarah was past the age of child bearing. So Sarah laughed to herself as she thought, "After I'm worn out and my master is old, will I now have this pleasure?" Then the Lord said to Abraham, "Why did Sarah laugh and say, 'Will I really have a child, now that I am old?' Is anything too hard for the Lord? I will return to you at the appointed time next year and Sarah will have a son." Sarah was afraid, so she lied and said, "I did not laugh," But he said, "Yes, you did laugh." (Genesis 18:9-15).

The fact is this was an impossible situation. Sarah laughed. But God had the last laugh, and Isaac was born. Abraham and Sarah named him Isaac. They named him *laughter.*

Encourage young adults to trust God for the how. *Lord, how am I going to make ends meet this month? Lord, how am I ever going to get out of debt? Lord, how are we ever going to be able to afford a home? Lord, how can I handle all of this pressure? Lord, how can I ever find time to spend with you?* As young adults learn to trust God for the how and the where, they learn to be willing to trust God for the who.

Why? A couple of months ago, I was walking through a hallway at church and noticed a beautiful little girl walking with her mom. She was so pretty, I felt compelled to point her out to my wife. A few weeks later I received a call to go to a house and visit a mother whose nine-year-old had been murdered. You got it—it was that little girl. Why?

As I write this, the area where I live is being terrorized by a sniper who shoots men, women, and children going about their daily lives. Why? Some things are unfathomable.

Abraham faced just such an unfathomable situation. After the promise of a child had finally been fulfilled, he was asked to sacrifice that very child. Why? Abraham had no idea that God wouldn't let him go through with it. Abraham didn't know that. He didn't have the Bible to teach him about what God's nature was really like. He had only the knowledge of what God had taught him in the where and the how of the promises God had already fulfilled.

> " As young adults learn to trust God for who *he* is, they will slowly learn to trust him for who *they* are. They will begin to understand their true identity in Christ. "

As disciples grow in their knowledge of God's nature by learning to trust him in the where and how of their lives, they'll begin to trust him for the why. We won't always understand everything—some things remain unfathomable. But we'll learn to trust and obey. As young adults learn to trust God for who *he* is, they will slowly learn to trust him for who *they* are. They will begin to understand their true identity in Christ.

OUR TRUE SELVES

My friend Trevor always comes across as tough, standoffish, and a little arrogant. A few months ago, he came to visit me for a couple of days and, through crazy circumstances, ended up having emergency surgery. Because of that, he had to stay at my house, on the couch in the great room, for a whole extra week. It was fun for me to see my family's reaction to Trevor's true self. They discovered he is warm, funny, and caring. After he left, he wrote each of the four of us a note to say thank you for taking care of him. My wife mentioned how different he was than what she had thought! Why is that?

It's because all of us are really made up of two selves. Paul Tournier, in his book *The Meaning of Persons,* calls these two selves the *person* and the *personage.* Each of us is a mixture of our true self (the person) and the self we show to others (the personage).

When I was a child, my mother used to take me to her church.

QUEStions

- How is your own private self different from the self you show others?
- Why do people keep their private selves hidden?
- How does this affect people on the quest for Christ?

Every Sunday the minister would give an invitation to accept Christ as Lord and Savior. After sitting there a number of Sundays, I decided it was time for me to join the folks raising their hands. I was on the front row, and the minister seemed to be looking right at me. At five, I understood it was time to "turn or burn"!

I raised my hand and called out "Yoo-hoo!" to get the pastor's attention. After all, he seemed to be ignoring my raised hand. My mother, mortified, grabbed my arm and pulled it down, whispering to me to be quiet. As I looked around, I caught one or two smiles, as if I had in some way brought a welcome relief from the weekly routine.

I tell this story not to pass judgment on the social or moral rightness or wrongness of my mother's response, but because it probably played a part in shaping my personage. After all, this story was told over and over again in my presence, always played for laughs. As a young kid, I didn't understand why my Mom had put my hand down. I didn't understand why I had to be quiet. I didn't understand why people laughed at the story. I did understand how much I wanted to be loved and accepted, and so my personage began to take shape. I began to take on the role of the clown who acted out for laughs and my mom's attention.

At that time in my life, all I could do was interpret my mom's reactions as rejection. I was learning that I would be awarded and accepted on the basis of what I did and not who I am. I learned I must change to be accepted. I was not confident that I would be accepted for who I am.

QUE8tions

- How has the desire to belong affected you?
- How has it affected the young adults you serve?
- Where should we find acceptance, belonging, and significance as Christians?
- How do we trade in our false ideas about identity and worth for the real thing that God offers?

I've come to discover that a personage, the self we show to others, does serve a purpose in our lives as we seek to belong. I've found that in our imperfect world, the personage helps us to elicit a positive response from the significant people in our lives. Our souls cry out, "Don't they like me the way I am?" But in seeking the acceptance we so desperately desire, we begin to discover, although not necessarily consciously, those personages or masks which bring the desired responses from those who matter to us.

When I first moved into my current office, I took a bunch of framed degrees, awards, and certificates that I'd acquired over the years, and put them all up on one wall of my office. They looked very impressive, even to me. Shortly, a co-worker walked in and said, "Oh look, the 'I love Rich' wall!" I took them all down the next day. My need to be accepted continues, and I find myself hoping that if people see what I've done, they will not only accept me without question, but love me as well.

Even though I still struggle and seek people's approval, I have worked hard to discover my true self. When I first entered into ministry, I tried to be Chuck Swindoll. I mimicked the models in ministry I admired: I tried to preach like them, I tried to dress like them, I tried to use words and phrases like them, and I even tried to hold my Bible the way they did. Finally, I quit trying to be like anybody else. I reminded myself that God "shaped me and made me" (Job 10:8) to be just the way I am. As you guide young adults into a deeper relationship with Christ, help them to separate the personage from the true self, knit in the womb by a loving Creator.

QUESTions

- How can you help young adults embrace their true selves as they pursue Christ? Be specific.

PART THREE ——————————————

TRAVEL TIPS

Ministry Guidelines and Ideas

Now it's time to devise programs to fit your church culture and geographic area. Creating programs from theory or out of a vacuum is difficult, so we want to show you how some other young adult ministries have worked out these dimensions. We'll look at examples from Mars Hill Fellowship in Seattle, Solomon's Porch in Minneapolis, Scum of the Earth in Denver, Graceland Ministry in Santa Cruz, and Frontline in Washington, D.C.

The information in this chapter will lead you to try, adapt, and create your own programs. Remember that programs are not an end in themselves. They're simply a method to help young adults on their journey of Christ formation. So before we begin with the specifics, let's begin with a few cautions.

CAUTIONS FOR YOUNG ADULT MINISTRY

Don't try to duplicate another ministry.

What works in one place may or may not work where you are. First Corinthians 12:4-6 says, "There are different kinds of gifts, but the same Spirit. There are different kinds of service, but the same Lord. There are different kinds of working, but the same God works all of them in all men." It's up to God what ministries you do, and it's up to God what effect your ministry has. You need to look to God to decide how to go about discipling young adults.

It's about excellence, not size.

The first question anyone asks us is "How many people come to Frontline?" It's easy to get puffed up and say, "Oh, we have X-number of people." But how many people come is not the most important thing about Frontline. Frontline is a ministry dedicated to excellence and to facilitating Christ formation in young adults.

Everything stands or falls on servant leadership.

The key to effective ministry is leadership, and the key to leadership is servanthood. Jesus told his disciples, "You've observed how godless rulers throw their weight around, how quickly a little power goes to their heads. It's not going to be that way with you. Whoever wants to be great must become a servant. Whoever wants to be first among you must be your slave. That is what the Son of Man has done: He came to serve, not be served—and then to give away his life in exchange for the many who are held hostage" (Matthew 20:25-28, *The Message*). Selfless leadership is servant leadership, and it's the most effective leadership style in facilitating Christ formation in others. Here are the six principles of servant leadership that we teach at Frontline.

Servant Leadership Principle 1: Humble your heart!
(Matthew 11:29; Luke 14:7-11; Philippians 2:3-4, *The Message*)

Servant Leadership Principle 2: Build a culture of high trust.
(Mark 10:32-41)

Servant Leadership Principle 3: Shepherd your team.
(Mark 10:45; John 10:11)

Servant Leadership Principle 4: Take risks!
(Hebrews 11:1)

Servant Leadership Principle 5: Share responsibility and authority.
(John 13:15; Ephesians 4:11-13)

Servant Leadership Principle 6: Build a team.
(Ecclesiastes 4:9-12; Luke 9:1-2)

Stewardship of people's gifts is critical.

Church leaders often act as if they alone are to do the work of ministry. But that's not what the Bible teaches. The Bible teaches that the job of the pastor is to equip people for ministry (Ephesians 4:12). This is especially critical when working with young adults. They have passion and a willingness to do something with their lives that counts. When you can help young adults line up their spiritual gifts and passions with the vision of your ministry, you have a dynamic combination that produces health and vibrancy in ministry.

GENERAL GUIDELINES FOR YOUNG ADULT MINISTRY

General Guideline 1: You must understand these principles of young adult culture.

Principle 1: Young adults prefer strong, same-age leaders.

Principle 2: Young adults place a premium on relationships.

Principle 3: Young adults want excellence not entertainment in the church. Any service or Sunday school class has to be "real," not phony. People must be authentic. Young adults respond to the use of story in teaching and preaching and more of the arts in times of corporate worship.

Principle 4: Young adults have an "ancient-future" orientation when it comes to time: They're comfortable with the high-tech digital world and also have a high degree of interest in the traditions of the past. TNL, a young adult church in Denver, uses this motto: "Creating a twenty-first century church with first-century truth."

Principle 5: Young adults are holistic. That is, they want to integrate all aspects of their lives with spirituality.

General Guideline 2: You need a philosophy of ministry statement.

Since young adults want ownership of any ministry they participate in, it's wise to have a clearly articulated philosophy of ministry. The following philosophy of ministry statement is from Frontline.

1. **The starting point of our ministry is God, not human activity.**
   "I planted the seed, Apollos watered it, but God made it grow" (1 Corinthians 3:6).

2. **The guide for our ministry is the Bible, not human wisdom.**
   "For my thoughts are not your thoughts, neither are my ways your ways," declares the Lord. As the heavens are higher than the earth, so are my ways higher than your ways and my thoughts than your thoughts. As the rain and the snow come down from heaven, and do not return to it without watering the earth and making it bud and flourish, so that it yields seed for the sower and bread for the eater, so is my word that goes out from my mouth: It will not return to me empty, but will accomplish what I desire and achieve the purpose for which I sent it" (Isaiah 55:8-11).

3. **The focus of our ministry is people, not programs.**
   "We loved you so much that we were delighted to share with you not only the gospel of God but our lives as well, because you had become so dear to us" (1 Thessalonians 2:8).
   "For God so loved the world that he gave his one and only Son, that whoever believes in him shall not perish but have eternal life" (John 3:16).

4. **The goal of our ministry is that everyone be a growing Christian, not just a believer.**
   "We proclaim him, admonishing and teaching everyone with all wisdom, so that we may present everyone perfect in Christ. To this end I labor, struggling with all his energy, which so powerfully works in me" (Colossians 1:28-29).

5. **The environment for our ministry is teamwork (the body working together, not people working individually).**

   "Just as each of us has one body with many members, and these members do not all have the same function, so in Christ we who are many form one body, and each member belongs to all the others. We have different gifts, according to the grace given us. If a man's gift is prophesying, let him use it in proportion to his faith. If it is serving, let him serve; if it is teaching, let him teach; if it is encouraging, let him encourage; if it is contributing to the needs of others, let him give generously; if it is leadership, let him govern diligently; if it is showing mercy, let him do it cheerfully" (Romans 12:4-8).

6. **The process of our ministry is spiritual reproduction, not only spiritual addition.**

   "And the things you have heard me say in the presence of many witnesses entrust to reliable men who will also be qualified to teach others" (2 Timothy 2:2).

General Guideline 3: You must understand the importance of vision.

A carefully constructed vision statement helps people know where your ministry is headed. It helps people understand what makes your ministry unique. Graceland Ministry, a church in Santa Cruz, California, (www.santacruzbible.org/graceland) provides a good example.

The Vision of Graceland

To see God transform us into a community of believers who will know and creatively express the ancient truths of the Bible to the world around us.

There is a lot of confusion among young adults about who Jesus is, and what true Christianity is all about. Our desire is to see Graceland be a unique place known in Santa Cruz County, which specifically is geared for new generations, and see thousands and thousands of those who have been raised with no biblical background and may not normally attend a church service find that they can identify with the music, the teaching style, and most of all, the community of people who attend. Our strategy to see this occur is not a systematic plan, but a relational and organic one.

General Guideline 4: You need core values.

Every ministry needs criteria to help it measure whether it's accomplishing its vision. Core values do that. Mars Hill Fellowship in Seattle (www.marshill.fm/) has articulated its core values very well. But before we show you its core values, it will be helpful to understand who it is as a ministry.

On its Web site, Mars Hill is defined as "a community of individuals with diverse backgrounds, personalities, philosophies, ideas, and visions; united by a relationship with Christ. Mars Hill is not 'church' the way our society defines it. Mars Hill is a family. A family with members of all ages, the majority of whom are in their twenties. In this family, some have an intimate relationship with God, others desire to know him better, and still others don't know him at all. This family gathers on Sunday nights to worship God, to pray, to learn, and for some, to just hang out. Mars Hill is essentially a family created by God for his glory."

Mars Hill Fellowship Core Values

Meaning

God is eternal and therefore gives meaning to every age, culture and worldview. For this reason, Mars Hill seeks to continually understand cultural and worldview shifts to effectively minister to new generations.

Beauty

God is beautiful and his creation reflects his beauty. God created man and woman in his image and likeness to also create works of beauty. For this reason, Mars Hill values the arts, expression, and creativity.

Truth

God is True and has made his Truth known in his Word and the person of Jesus Christ. For this reason, Mars Hill seeks to know, live, and proclaim Truth out of a love for God.

Community

God exists in a perfect community of Father, Son, and Holy Spirit and created men and women to also live in community. For this reason, Mars Hill seeks to model deep and personal faith by serving others in a loving and authentic community.

General Guideline 5: You need to define your target group.

Another critical element to consider before developing your programs is to understand who it is you are trying to reach. Let's take a look at one church, Scum of the Earth Church (http://somegirl.hxc.com/scum.html), that has done an excellent job in clearly defining its target.

Associate pastor Reese Roper says, "Scum of the Earth is a church in Denver, Colorado, that was started by Five Iron Frenzy. It's an outreach to people that have been ostracized by mainstream Christianity—Punks, Goths, Skaters, Five Iron Frenzy fans, and former quarterbacks of the Baltimore Ravens."

The pastors and leaders of Scum of the Earth sensed a biblical calling to these ostracized people of the urban jungles and find the basis of this calling in 1 Corinthians 4:11-13: "To this very hour we go hungry and thirsty, we are in rags, we are brutally treated, we are homeless. We work hard with our own hands. When we are cursed, we bless; when we are persecuted, we endure it; when we are slandered, we answer kindly. Up until this moment we have become the scum of the earth, the refuse of the world."

Scum of the Earth Vision Statement

We strive to be a church who
- seeks intimacy with God and honest relationships with others,
- cultivates creativity and uses everyone's gifts,
- asks questions while seeking Truth,
- recognizes our need for a Savior,
- passionately yet respectfully shares the saving love of Christ, and
- demonstrates God's love in our community.

Scum of the Earth Beginnings

They began a church for the tattooed, pierced, and neon-hair crowd who are either unwelcome in a traditional church setting or unable to get out of bed on Sunday mornings for a religion that seems irrelevant to their daily lives.

Church Name Concerns

In a conversation with Rich, one of the pastors made the following comments in regard to the name of the church.

> It doesn't sound like a church name…on purpose. We really want to connect with people who have no interest in "church" by society's definition. There are plenty of churches for 'normal people,' and we think we have a unique calling to reach out to our otherwise unreached friends. Our name is integral to that process. Whether outcast by society—punks, skaters, ravers, homeless people—or by the church itself, many who come can identify with the name Scum of the Earth since they have been previously treated as such.
>
> More important to us, however, the name implies that being people of faith does not mean we are better than anyone else. We know many non-Christians who think Christians are out to cast judgment on them. Our name makes it clear that we aren't about that. We are just aware of our need for God as "scum of the earth." Fortunately, God never sees us like that! But the name is humble and we like that.

Churches like Scum of the Earth have a very specific target group. Knowing their target group well helps them know what to do as well as what not to do as they make plans to reach and disciple young adults.

General Guideline 6: You need variety in your ministry.

It's important to fully integrate a person's quest for Christ through very creative ways. Solomon's Porch (www.solomonsporch.com) in Minneapolis is a good example of a church that provides an integrated ministry. An integrated ministry is mindful of the fact that all areas of life are connected, including faith, time, family, work, body, money, and intellect.

The Vision of Solomon's Porch

Our belief is that God intends Christianity be a way of life which sends us into the world to serve God and our neighbors so that God's will may be done on earth as it is in heaven. The church is never to be the withdrawn or isolated end-user of the gospel of Jesus. Rather we receive it so that we may be equipped and sent into the world to love our neighbors and serve "the least of these." In this sense, Solomon's Porch doesn't *have* a mission; it *is* mission. As Christians we see ourselves as a growing people who are learning to live life with God in the way of Jesus. We represent a generous orthodoxy, rooted in the Scriptures and consistent with the ancient creeds of the church. We desire to share life with one another in such a way that we become a living, breathing, local expression of the global, historical body of Christ.

FRONTLINE'S VISION AND CORE VALUES

The Vision of Frontline

To help young adults go to the next level in their spiritual journeys with Jesus Christ. This vision is built upon 2 Peter 3:18a: "Grow in grace and understanding of our Master and Savior, Jesus Christ" *(The Message)*.

The Six Core Values of Frontline

1. To create a safe environment for young adults to experience God.

For those who have yet to decide to follow Jesus Christ, we desire that they come to understand that they are valued and loved by God for who they are, not for what they do. We believe that each person has worth because they are made in the image and likeness of God and because Jesus Christ died for them. We want each person to experience this value and love in an environment that is accepting, nonjudgmental, and committed to his or her personal needs. We emphasize not only knowing "about" God, but personally "knowing" God.

2. To help young adults identify their calling and use their gifts to help others.

We believe that God has given each follower of Christ a gift(s) and a unique calling to do ministry and serve others. As people act on their calling by using their gifts to serve others, we believe that they will grow in their relationship with Jesus.

3. To build biblically functioning communities of young adults to help them develop a strong, intimate relationship with God and each other.

We believe that life change is most facilitated within the context of community where followers of Christ live out the "One Another" commands of Scripture. We desire that each young adult be cared for and challenged within the context of a small group. A biblical community embraces people both in times of celebration and crisis; it's a place where they can share fears, dreams, failures, and pain without fearing rejection.

A biblical community strives to facilitate the development of healthy, intimate relationships with God, each other, ourselves, and those in our world.

4. To help each young adult develop a biblical worldview.

We desire to facilitate the process of God changing lives and developing godly character through a growing value system based on the Bible. A biblical worldview is one that perceives the world from God's perspective and is able to address the challenges that present themselves outside of this context.

5. To implement effective strategies to influence young adults who have yet to follow Christ.

We want to open the doors to those who have yet to follow Christ. We want to help them understand that God loves them and desires a relationship with them through Jesus Christ. We desire to use culturally relevant means to communicate the eternal truths of God in ways that those in our culture will understand and embrace.

6. To equip young adults for godly living through mentoring relationships.

Our desire is that each young adult comes to imitate the lifestyle and practices of Jesus Christ with the focus on becoming a fully devoted follower in all areas of life: spiritually, emotionally, and physically. We believe an effective means that facilitates this process is one-to-one mentoring in which a more mature follower of Christ comes alongside a younger follower to personally instruct him or her in the ways of the Lord.

TRANSFORMATIONAL COMMUNITIES

In our book *Getting Real,* we discuss how to develop a ministry of small groups that facilitates biblical community. Since writing that book, we have further developed our small-group processes. In this section, we'd like to update you on our leadership recruitment and development systems to further your effectiveness at facilitating biblical community with your young adults.

Recruiting New Small-Group Leaders

Recruiting new leaders is one of the biggest challenges faced by growing small-group ministries. The best way to recruit new leaders is to develop a reproductive model of ministry in which apprenticeship (and multiple apprenticeships) is encouraged. If one depends on recruiting leaders for growth, the ministry is destined to fail. A reproductive model is not only a biblical model but is also the most effective way to do ministry.

Small-Group Leadership Approval Process

At Frontline we have a clear leadership approval process. The process begins with an application. The application covers the leadership candidate's spiritual background, ministry background, personal strengths, and weaknesses. Along with the application, three references are required from people other than family members who know the applicant well and have possibly done ministry with them previously. Both the application and the reference forms help us to know best how to lead each of the individuals entering our team. Once the application and references are completed, the leadership candidate has an interview with a staff member or a coach. Remember, a coach is simply a leader who oversees three or four other small-group leaders. At this interview, our vision and values are discussed, and many of the same issues covered in the application are addressed. Meeting with people personally allows for people skills to be observed.

New Leader Training

New leaders and apprentices (an apprentice is a leader-in-training, not an assistant) are equipped through a one-day, six-hour training seminar.

This seminar covers a combination of group philosophy and hands-on leadership skills in an interactive format. It's held regularly (six times a year). Leaders are not required to attend training before they begin their group. In fact, many leaders get more out of the training if they have led their group for a month or two before attending.

Ongoing Small-Group Leader Training

1. Coaching

Coaching is our key strategy for ongoing small-group leader training. Coaches invest in three to four leaders so that the leaders grow personally, spiritually, and in leadership skills. Coaches invest in leaders through one-on-one meetings, huddles (small groups), and group visits. Coaching allows our ministry to remain decentralized and relational at the same time.

2. VHS

At VHS (vision, huddle, and skill building), leaders are equipped with leadership skills and re-energized by hearing the LDG vision. (Leadership Development Group is the name we have given to our small-group ministry at Frontline.) Leaders are also reinforced with vital relationships as they meet with their coaches and other leaders. At Frontline we hold this meeting the first Sunday night of the month during one of the services.

3. Online Resources for Leaders

Providing resources online has given us a "virtual notebook" for our leaders. (You can find these resources at www.frontline.to. But you will need a password for access. We keep our leader area password protected so that the area is secure and safe to share all levels of the ministry. To acquire your temporary password, please e-mail your request to Mike Hurt at Mhurt@mcleanbible.org.) Here, up-to-date articles and training materials are posted. Also leaders can research curriculum choices and read others' thoughts regarding curriculum that has or hasn't worked in their groups. In addition to resources, the site allows leaders to update rosters and view current leadership directories.

4. Small-Group Connection

Following many years of trying to find the best way to integrate new-comers into Frontline small groups, we've settled on what we call the Small-Group Connect meeting. This is now our only entry point for group life. Following every Frontline service, the connect meeting is held to cast the small-group vision, prep people for the "normal" small-group meeting, and explain the placement process. The connect meeting is also a great place to recruit new leaders because many people entering our ministry have previous leadership experience and have not been asked to serve yet at Frontline.

With these updated processes, in addition to our in-depth discussion of small groups in *Getting Real,* you'll be equipped to build this key dimension of ministry to facilitate Christ formation in your young adult ministry.

Finally, we want to show you some practical programs that we use at Frontline to facilitate the service dimensions of Christ formation.

SERVICE

Serving others is an important element of Christ formation. Jesus said, "For I was hungry and you gave me something to eat, I was thirsty and you gave me something to drink, I was a stranger and you invited me in, I needed clothes and you clothed me, I was sick and you looked after me, I was in prison and you came to visit me" (Matthew 25:35-36).

God is pleased when we serve others through acts of compassion. At Frontline we provide a variety of opportunities for young adults to live out dreams for God through acts of service toward others. We divide our service projects into two primary categories: domestic service projects and international short-term mission projects.

Domestic Service Projects

When we say domestic service projects, we simply mean that we go out into our community to live out the truths of God's Word by serving people instead of trying to prove God's existence by means of fine-sounding arguments. You can read more about service evangelism in Steve Sjogren's book *Conspiracy of Kindness.*

In our own book *Getting Real,* we provide great ideas that give young adults opportunities to serve as well as share Christ with others. You can read all about these service projects in our first book. In addition, we have added a very unique component to our domestic service projects that we do want to tell you about: It's called IntenCITY. It's a road trip with a purpose.

IntenCITY

Putting a spin on the MTV show *Road Rules,* we send twenty Frontliners on a wild ride called IntenCITY, which involves taking young adults to three to five different locations in nine days. We don't tell the participants where they're going or what they'll be doing. The purpose of each experience is twofold. We want to promote an outward focus, sharing God's love in real and practical ways with those met on the journey through various means of service; and an inward focus, learning to put full control of ourselves and our plans in God's hands and not rely on our own strength.

Who: We divided into two teams of ten people each, equally divided between men and women. One man and one woman from each team are designated the group leaders. Participants are selected through an application and interview process (similar to the way we select small-group leaders).

Because we were asking people to be completely "in the dark" about where they were going and what was going to happen to them, the idea drew a crowd that was flexible and easygoing.

What: The activities vary. We have conducted children's day camps with inner city ministries; shared Christ with tourists and athletes at the 2002 Winter Olympics; provided construction workers to help with a hurricane relief team; handed out lunches with a homeless shelter program; took a prayer walk around Harlem; led an evangelistic worship service; and did spring cleaning to surprise a houseful of missionary interns who were away at a conference.

Where: Any place where people can serve and be out of their comfort zones.

When: Most trips are nine days and run from a Friday to a Sunday.

How: Each team member was asked to raise money for the trip and participate in a group fund-raiser to build team dynamics and support the cost of the trip.

Team Dynamics: The team had five meetings before the trip to build cohesiveness and settle logistics. Each team member was paired with a same-sex prayer partner and an anonymous encourager of the opposite sex.

Results: Although working with a ministry only one day can make authentic relationships outside the group nearly impossible,

God is gracious and used these teams to genuinely encourage the ministries we came in contact with. Even the long hours together are a blessing since they afforded team members the opportunity to get to know each other with very few distractions. But the best part of the trips was seeing the team members step out of their comfort zones, and let God shine through them.

How to Get Started With Your Own IntenCITY

Initial questions you need to answer:

1. What's the vision behind the trip? What are you hoping to accomplish—stretching the people on the team? evangelism? sharing God's love in practical ways through service?

2. How many people do you want to take?

3. What's your budget? Money will guide many of your decisions in planning the trip. How will you raise the money? Will you ask for church budget funds? hold fund-raisers? expect participants to raise their own support?

4. How many sites do you want to visit? Will the sites be local or across the country?

5. What's the team process going to be? This includes application/interview process, pre-trip team meetings, team building, time for processing while on the trip, and follow-up once the team has returned.

Once you've answered some of these general questions, you're ready to focus on the four main areas of the trip planning: housing, service opportunities, transportation, and meals. The best way to line up opportunities to serve as well as the other travel logistics is through networking. Here are some general ideas for each aspect of the trip.

Housing

- Church floors (Throw some sleeping bags down, and you're good to go.)
- Housing provided on work project site
- Hotel

- College campus
- Youth hostels (www.hiayh.org)

Service Opportunities
- Social ministry, such as a homeless ministry or crisis pregnancy clinic
- Construction and labor ministry, such as Habitat for Humanity or a neighborhood cleanup project
- International ministry, such as a port or refugee ministry
- Creative evangelism, such as beach outreach, campus outreach, or "full-service" gas station and other random acts of kindness
- Children's ministry or seniors' ministry, such as vacation Bible school or senior care facilities

Transportation
- Church vans
- Carpools
- Rental vehicles
- Buses
- Trains
- Airplanes

Meals
- Cook on your own (We divided our first team into serving teams, and one of them was responsible for cooking several meals while we were on the trip.)
- Provided by the worksite (Some sites are very accommodating!)
- Restaurants

Helpful Hints
1. Have directions, phone numbers, and all pertinent information to every location and worksite before you leave. You don't want to have to track the information down once you are on the road.

2. Use cell phones or walkie-talkies between vehicles as you travel. These are invaluable both for team building and for practicality when you run into snags.

3. Don't take shortcuts on team building or follow-up! We do five pre-trip meetings and an overnight retreat, and they're all important to help the team get to know each other and get ready to serve together. Follow-up is critical so that you don't lose the spiritual momentum of the trip. Encourage team members to get involved in service once they get home or explore a call that God may have placed in their life.

4. Don't underestimate the power of the "simple" projects. Handing out bag lunches to the homeless in the innercity or pumping gas at a local gas station can have a profound impact on your team and the community!

5. Only the trip planner and team leaders get all of the details. We usually go day by day with our team members. They're on a need-to-know basis. This is a stretch for some and freeing for others.

6. If at first you don't "succeed," try, try again! It takes some time to get in the groove of trip planning, especially when you can't tell the team the details. This can also make team meetings interesting. And sometimes on the trip, plans get out of whack or just don't go as well as you would have hoped. Don't let that set you back. This is a great experience for your people!

These IntenCITYS have become a very exciting part of our domestic outreach projects.

Global Impact Teams

A Global Impact team is a short-term, international missions trip. We believe the Bible calls for all Christians to be missionaries. From cover to cover, we see that God is at work in the world to restore the lost relationship with people from all the nations for his glory. However, it's also important to provide a biblical support for the strategies used in our attempt to accomplish global missions. The verses that follow provide our biblical basis for why and how we do missions at Frontline.

Biblical Foundations for Frontline Global Impact Trips

"As the father has sent me, I am sending you" (John 20:21b).

"By this all men will know that you are my disciples, if you love one another" (John 13:35).

"Go into all the world and preach the good news to all creation" (Mark 16:15).

"Therefore go and make disciples of all nations" (Matthew 28:19).

"Ask the Lord of the harvest, therefore, to send out workers into his harvest field" (Matthew 9:38).

These statements show God's heart for the world—the world he sent his Son to die for! We get to see God's plan for the world explode right before our eyes in the book of Acts. In Acts the groundwork is laid by the Holy Spirit to build the church globally–not just locally! This is made even clearer by the epistles that show the church multiplying in new areas. Paul said, "I am not ashamed of the gospel, because it is the power of God for the salvation of everyone who believes" (Romans 1:16a), and he proclaimed it to the end of his life.

The short-term missions trips that make up our Global Impact program may seem far from this level of missions intensity, and we do have far to go. But our heart is to provide opportunities for Frontliners to catch this passion and to truly find God's leading in their own lives through the life change that occurs on these trips. We want to be carrying out God's desires and Christ's commands.

Global Impact is built on a solid theology of missions. In addition these trips provide a rich opportunity for community among team members. I often tell people: "When you go into a Third World context with a group of people, you become family whether you want to or not." Therefore, it's important to build strong community on our teams. Here is how we do that.

Important Elements to Ensure a Successful Global Impact Trip
Element 1: Developing relationships among team members.

Building community begins five months before the trip. During this time, five mandatory meetings are required of each team member. These meetings serve as a catalyst in unifying the team members. Each meeting is three to four hours long, giving ample time to get to know each other. During the five months, each member must share his or her faith story in detail with the rest of the group. If they have never done this before, we help them write it out. This serves two purposes. One, it allows others on the team to get to know them very personally; and two, if the trip involves evangelism, being able to share one's faith story is a key tool when sharing Christ with others. Each team meeting also involves a time of corporate prayer for one another's needs.

Element 2: Raising Funds

Each team member is also required to raise the necessary funds to pay for his or her part of the trip's cost. This also lends itself to building a sense of community as they raise money through work projects and fund-raisers. Nothing builds a sense of team spirit like rolling up your sleeves and sweating together. Fund-raisers let the team see God's hand at work on its behalf as they work together to raise support. Fund-raisers also raise the value of the trip in the mind of the team. Work projects let the team see how each person contributes to the team. These projects help team members begin to grow accustomed to each other's personalities, too.

Element 3: Leadership

Giving leadership responsibilities to team members gives them an opportunity to see how they are valued by and valuable to the team. It gives team members an opportunity to support and encourage one another as they succeed and make mistakes in their tasks.

Element 4: Maintaining the sense of community in the field.

It's critical that relationships are nurtured and sustained on the trip. One way to ensure this is to have team meetings on the field. These allow the team members to share in one another's experiences. These meetings provide a safe environment to process any fears or frustrations and allow the team leader time to refocus on the "task at hand" if necessary.

Element 5: Making the team have fun!

Every trip has a mandatory time of "R & R" prior to returning home. This takes the focus off the cross-cultural experiences and helps the team unite and grow.

Element 6: Preparing for re-entry shock.

Returning to the States can be a difficult transition for some of the team members. In order to minimize this, we suggest the following.

1. Reunite the team as a single unit prior to returning.
2. Maintain relationships even after the trip is officially over.
3. Provide opportunities for team members to share their stories with others.
4. Require follow-up meetings. These help to remind the team what they experienced together.
5. Do ministry together after the trip, such as local service projects.
6. Provide a way, if possible, for team members to stay in touch with the nationals from the site you visited.

Frequently
Asked Questions

1. Don't all young adults deal with a lot of the same issues, whether they came of age in the 1940s, 1960s, 1980s, or today?

From a developmental perspective, all young adults deal with similar issues. They all go through a season where they struggle with their own identity and the issue of making their faith their own instead of something that was handed down to them by their parents. All young adults experience the trials of defining their purpose and unique place in life. These and other issues are not unique to today's postmodern young adults. However, what makes today's young adults unique is the extent to which various forces have shaped them.

Forces That Have Shaped Today's Young Adults
Divorce
Conservative statistics estimate that 40 percent of today's young adults come from broken homes, and the pain this causes has left its mark on this generation. Divorce is not a unique experience for this generation, but the overwhelming number of people who have experienced the pain of broken families is.

Anti-Child Sentiment
Simply put, children born and raised during the 1970s were considered a bother and an impediment to an adult's freedom to do whatever he or she wanted. As a result, children experienced a wide variety of societal

discrimination. There was also a growing fear among many people in the United States that population growth was becoming a serious threat to food resources. Many books published during this time sounded the alarm, such as *The Case Against Having Children, Life Without Birth,* and *The Baby Trap.* All in all, today's young adults have been deeply scarred by this discrimination.

The Meltdown of the Traditional Family

During the 1960s and into the 1970s, the women's liberation movement was in full swing. As a result, traditional family roles, such as the stay-at-home mom, were questioned and, in many cases, looked upon with contempt as a form of gender inequality and oppression. Fathers' roles also changed in light of the women's liberation movement, as women felt less economically dependent on men. The pill also made it possible for people to have more sexual attachments without forming families. With legalized abortion, babies in the womb became fetuses—extensions of someone else, not precious creations in their own right.

Economic Uncertainty

Several factors have led to increasing unrest among young adults, including higher taxes in light of the aging baby boom population, uncertainty about whether Social Security contributions will be available at retirement, and low-paying jobs on top of pressing financial debt loads from student loans and credit cards. It's true that economic uncertainty is not unique to young adults today, but credit cards are offered to college students at an unprecedented rate, and that often leads to early credit debt and a lifetime of fiscal instability.

Global Distress

It's not that younger generations in the past have not experienced global distress, however the access to this information via the Internet, CNN, CNBC, and others make the information so readily available that one almost can't get away from it. As a result, this mass of constant distressing information exacerbates a young person's sense of hopelessness and despair.

The massive scale of recent events such as 9/11 and the subsequent daily threat of terrorism worldwide add to this in ways not experienced by previous generations.

Fatherless America

Many of today's young adults grew up with absentee fathers, and that has made its mark on this generation in respect to healthy gender identification and development.

The Internet

Many of today's young adults were the first generation in history to grow up with the Internet. There has not been enough time to test the implications of this fully, but there are some concerns of the negative consequences of life with the Internet, including impersonal communication and access to potentially harmful material without benefit of traditional social filters.

Cultural Diversity

America has become a pluralistic society in which every race and religion provides information that must be sifted through in order to determine our beliefs and values.

Devaluation of Life

The tragic events at Columbine High School in Littleton, Colorado, reveal that violence is on the rise and much more prevalent today than it has ever been. The value of life is on the decline: Abortion continues and euthanasia issues abound, while cloning and stem cell research combine to cast a dark shadow on the value of life.

These issues have largely shaped values, attitudes, and behavior. In light of these issues, we think you'll agree that today's young adults have personal issues and ethical choices that make them unique among past generations. And as a result, discipleship with today's young adults must be different.

2.   What's discipleship?

The term *discipleship* has a variety of meanings. Most Christians think of discipleship as a one-on-one relationship in which a more mature Christian comes alongside a new Christian and helps him or her understand the basic elements of the Christian faith. This use of the word *discipleship* implies there's a leader and a follower, a teacher and a student.

In this book, we have often used the term discipleship to describe the life-long quest of every Christian to become progressively more like Jesus Christ through sanctification. In those places in which we speak of one person discipling others, we have in mind a more holistic methodology. The teaching relationship between discipler and disciple is just a small part. Thus, we see a more comprehensive process of discipleship facilitated through the four dimensions of worship, community, maturity, and service.

3.   What is Christ formation?

Within today's postmodern culture, the word *spiritual* has a very broad definition and might include many things that we would not agree with. For example, to be spiritual doesn't necessarily mean being a Christian or even having faith in God; it can simply mean believing in something beyond oneself. A spiritual person might identify with one of the major world religions, mother earth, or any number of things.

Years ago a term like spiritual formation was understood in one certain way, but not today. We've been intentional in choosing the term Christ formation in order to eliminate any confusion over what we're talking about. Christ formation is the process by which a Christian becomes more like Christ as God transforms him or her into the image of Jesus. In Romans 8:29a, Paul tells us that this is God's plan for those he calls: "For those God foreknew he also predestined to be conformed to the likeness of his Son." As a result, after a person comes to saving faith in Christ through repentance, God's principal agenda for the rest of his or her life is this process we are calling Christ formation.

4.   Why do I have to make disciples; why can't I just evangelize?

Two reasons. First, we are commanded to make disciples by Jesus himself. Matthew 28:19a says clearly: "Therefore go and make disciples of all nations." Second, making disciples is the most effective means of evangelism.

It all boils down to the multiplication factor. If you win five people to Christ and train and disciple them in a small group for one year and then each of the five goes and does the same, the numbers escalate rapidly. The reality is, you'll win more people to Christ by using the model of discipleship that we have talked about in this book than you will by doing evangelism alone. Perhaps that's why Jesus commanded us to make disciples, because that's the most effective means of evangelism.

5.   Aren't the words *disciple* and *Christian* synonymous?

The Bible seems to show a clear distinction between these two terms. In fact, Jesus' teachings on discipleship and salvation are quite distinct. In John 3:16, 6:28-29, and 11:25, Jesus clearly taught that saving faith was the result of belief and trust. A person becomes a Christian by believing in Christ. A disciple on the other hand is a person who has made a conscious decision to follow Christ and to pattern a lifestyle after his. Jesus summarized the profile of a disciple as follows:

A disciple is willing to deny self, take up his or her cross, and follow Christ (Luke 9:23-25).

A disciple puts Christ first: before self, family, material possessions, and friends (Luke 14:26-27).

A disciple is committed to Christ's teaching and obeys his commands (John 8:31).

A disciple is committed to spreading the gospel (Matthew 9:36-38).

A disciple loves other people just as Jesus does (John 13:34-35).

A disciple bears much fruit (John 15:8).

Jesus clearly stated that a person not willing to commit to these elements could not be his disciple (Luke 14:33), but he did not say that such a person was not saved. These are the various elements that define a disciple in Jesus' mind. Passages such as Hebrews 5:11-13 and 1 Corinthians 3:1-3, 10-15 make it clear that a person can truly be saved and be going to heaven yet not bear fruit in this life. Therefore, we believe that the words *Christian* and *disciple* don't necessarily mean the same thing.

6. When you use the phrase "quest for Christ," do you imply the disciple plays a role in the Christ-formation process?

A quest is simply a journey with a purpose. For a believer in Christ, the quest is his or her spiritual journey toward maturity in Christ. This journey is a lifelong endeavor to submit oneself to God's transformation process. As a person becomes more like Christ, those traits referred to as the fruit of the Spirit (Galatians 5:22-23) become more and more manifest. It's important to understand that a Christian cannot develop these character traits alone—they are produced by the Spirit's work in his or her life.

Notwithstanding, each Christian does have a part to play. In Ephesians 5:18 we are commanded to "be filled with the Spirit." The Greek tense implies that we are to be continually and habitually filled with the Spirit, stressing a daily action. The passive voice is most likely a permissive passive, which refers to the fact that being filled with the Spirit is something that Christians must allow to happen to them.

In other words, God will not force himself upon someone. A Christian must submit to God's character-changing process. But this word is also an imperative. An imperative is a command. We are commanded to "be filled with the Spirit." Therefore, a Christian must do something to facilitate this filling process. We believe that the command is to allow the Holy Spirit to control our lives, to submit to whatever God brings our way, knowing that he will use whatever happens to us for his glory and our transformation into the character of Christ.

7. What are some biblical examples of discipleship training?

Jesus is the best example. It's interesting to note that Jesus didn't do one-on-one discipleship training. Instead he trained the disciples in the context of a small community. As the disciples lived with Jesus, he used the four dimensions of discipleship to train them to be like him.

Jesus modeled a lifestyle of worship in that he lived his life for the glory of God and in accordance to the will of God. Jesus said in John 17:1,

"Glorify your Son, that your Son may glorify you" and in John 8:28-29, "I do nothing on my own but speak just what the Father has taught me. The one who sent me is with me; he has not left me alone, for I always do what pleases him." Jesus modeled for the disciples a life centered in God.

Jesus modeled self-care by taking time for solitude and prayer. Jesus also modeled a lifestyle of community by calling the twelve and living in constant contact with them. Finally, Jesus modeled compassion by giving of himself to others through teaching, healing, and dying on the cross for our sins.

8. What does the finished product of a disciple look like?

Becoming like Jesus Christ is a lifelong process that will not be complete until we die and are with him. First John 3:2 says: "Dear friends, now we are children of God, and what we will be has not yet been made known. But we know that when he appears, we shall be like him, for we shall see him as he is."

However, a Christian can progress in Christlikeness and even though that progress will not be completed in this life, a significant amount of progress can be made. The way Christians measure their progress is in their growing capacity to love. In 1 Corinthians 13:4-8a, Paul says: "Love is patient, love is kind. It does not envy, it does not boast, it is not proud. It is not rude, it is not self-seeking, it is not easily angered, it keeps no record of wrongs. Love does not delight in evil but rejoices with the truth. It always protects, always trusts, always hopes, always perseveres. Love never fails."

When we commit ourselves to living a life of love as Jesus did, these elements of love manifest themselves in our lives. Therefore, even though complete Christ formation is not possible in this life, progress can be made as a disciple pursues and lives a life of love.

9. How do I train other disciple makers?

You have to choose the right kind of people. When choosing the right kind of people, keep the following things in mind:

Pray. Prayer is important in the selection process. Jesus spent the whole night in prayer before choosing the twelve disciples (Luke 6:12-13).

Choose people you think can reproduce themselves into others.
This multiplication process cannot be overstated. When you choose a person who will in turn choose another and so on, you create a discipleship engine that eventually develops hundreds of disciples.

When choosing people for your discipleship group, take your time.
Watch people in action. Ask others about them. Do they have a good reputation? Are they people of integrity and character? Are they reliable? Reliability is perhaps the most important quality to look for as you choose people to be in your group. The multiplication process will break down if you choose unreliable people.

10. Why is it important to use movie clips as illustrations? Isn't that just entertaining people?

One of the important things to keep in mind in teaching is that people learn differently. There are three primary learning styles: visual, auditory, and kinesthetic. In any teaching environment like a worship service, Sunday school class, or small group, you want to utilize methods that connect with these three distinct learning styles.

Auditory learners need only to hear things for the lesson to stick. (Most traditional services favor this type of learning style.) Kinesthetic learners learn best through touch and motion. Tools that facilitate kinesthetic learners would include outlines and props similar to what we described in the Frontline communion services. Visual learners learn best when they see something as it relates to the lesson.

Whether by training or disposition, many of today's young adults are visual learners. Attend a concert where the live action is projected on a screen behind the performers and notice how many in the audience are actually focused on the screen rather than the live performer in front of them! We use movie clips to capitalize on this preference. Other tools that facilitate visual learners are Powerpoint presentations, props that illustrate your point, and dramas.

11. You talk about how to create a church that connects with young adults, but I'm not a pastor. I'm an individual who wants to help a postmodern young adult on his or her quest. What should I do? How is it different from the discipleship I've done with other individuals?

Again, our four dimensions of discipleship are nothing new or original. These are eternal principles that facilitate the process of Christ formation in a Christian's life. However if you keep these things in mind, whether you're a pastor or not, you'll be instrumental in the further development of your disciple/friend.

• View your relationship as a friendship as opposed to a teacher/student relationship. A friendship is reciprocal—you learn from each other and help and support each other. These are essential differences. Let your disciple/friend see your weaknesses and how you deal with them.

• Remember, more is caught than taught. Your lifestyle will teach your disciple/friend more than anything else you do. Your life should act as a commentary on the Scriptures.

• Focus on the four dimensions of discipleship (worship, self-care, community, and compassion) without making one a priority more than the others. Remember, traveling through all four dimensions provides a more complete perspective to the developing faith of new Christians.

• We suggest you focus the study and discussion on the Bible instead of on outside curriculum, especially if the people are brand-new Christians. Let them begin with a book of the Bible, such as 1 John or the gospel of John, and then discuss their questions together. We have found that the Holy Spirit really works in a new Christian's life as they read large portions of Scripture.

For example, Ken is in a discipling relationship with five guys. One of the guys, James, loves to read. Ken had James read through the gospel of

John and told him to write down any questions he wanted to discuss. At their next meeting, James told Ken that he had read through the gospel twice. The first time he read through it, he had pages of questions. Then as he read through it again, he answered half of his own questions.

It's amazing how the Holy Spirit enlightens a Christian's mind and gives him or her a new capacity to understand Scripture. We believe it's also important that you have the new Christian read from a modern translation such as The New International Version, The New Living Translation, or *The Message*. This will also help people understand what they are reading. We also believe that another important reason to have young Christians read the Bible primarily as the source of knowledge is that it familiarizes them with the Bible and takes away much of the intimidation people feel when they are new to the faith.

• Remember not to bury new Christians in tons of information. New Christians, especially if they have come to faith later in life, are overwhelmed with the magnitude and implications of their new life in Christ. They often find their new way of life is like trying to take a drink from a fire hydrant. Don't forget: Discipleship is a quest, a lifelong journey. You are just coming alongside new Christians for a particular phase of their journey with Christ.

12. How is discipleship relational?

When Jesus recruited his disciples, his invitation to them was "Come, follow me" (Matthew 4:19). In essence, Jesus was saying, "Hey guys, come do life with me, come see how I live out the teachings of the prophets, come watch how I live the life that results in meaning and glorifies God."

Jesus began his ministry with the disciples relationally by inviting them to do life with him. It was in the context of these relationships that Jesus taught them how to live a life that pleases the Father. That's why we won't be as effective in making disciples if we minimize the discipling process by reducing it to a program or to simply teaching a body of biblical knowledge.

When I invite people to enter into my world, I share with them my dreams, fears, and failures. In essence, I remove any real or perceived hierarchy and communicate that I'm a fellow traveler on the quest for Christ. What makes me different from them is that I've just been on the journey a little longer, and hopefully I can share what I've learned about God through my life. Discipleship is a relational process where we "do life together," and as a result we grow in Christlikeness.

13.   How do you create community?

Building a sense of community must be the passion and the commitment of the leader! For community to be truly effective, leaders need to have experienced the power of community themselves.

Frontline is driven by relationships. I (Ken) talk about the importance of relationships all the time. In my messages I often say things like "You can't do life alone, it's impossible" or "God created us for relationships— a relationship with him first and then with people."

I model the importance of relationships with the Frontline staff. At our staff meeting every other week, we discuss a book that we're all reading together. Each person facilitates a chapter from the book. We also spend a lot of time together. When a new blockbuster movie comes out, such as *Star Wars* or *Lord of the Rings,* I'll shut the office down for the afternoon and take the staff to the movies. Then we often come to my house to eat together and just hang out.

Community is not just a program where we try to get people involved. It must be a deeply held conviction by the leader. Community is a philosophy of ministry that has to be the core issue that you emphasize.

Recently the father of a Frontline associate pastor died unexpectedly. The father had lived about three hours away in Pennsylvania. On the day of the funeral, I shut down the Frontline office and the entire staff (all thirteen of us) drove to Pennsylvania to be with our friend. And not only did the staff go, but many of this pastor's volunteer leadership team were there as well. In the small congregation that gathered for the funeral, half were Frontliners from nearly two hundred miles away. It was a powerful demonstration of community that many of this pastor's family noticed and commented on.

If you want to build community, commitment to healthy relationships must be the most important aspect of your ministry, and the leader must model the type of commitment he or she wants to see from others.

14.   How do I get young adults passionate about small groups?

Young adults are busy. They have active social lives, and many put in long hours at work. Yet if you have made community an important element of the ethos of your church, and you create the right type of environment, young adults will join a small group. When I teach at conferences or when other churches visit Frontline, they marvel at how many young adults we have in small groups. Of the two thousand people who come on any given Sunday night to our two services, we have over sixteen hundred who meet in weekly or biweekly small groups. That's a staggering percentage. How did we get this going? Here are some of our secrets.

Secret 1: Leaders must create a culture of community. Relationships must be central to the philosophy of ministry. God created people to need him and each other; we cannot make it in life alone. And as we have talked about so much in this book, people cannot grow in Christ without grace and truth. Relationships are the primary vehicle that facilitate this.

Secret 2: Leaders must be in small groups. The power of genuine leadership cannot be overstated. Credibility is critical to leading young adults today. How can a leader talk about the value of small groups if they are not participating in them?

Secret 3: Talk about small groups all the time. Talk about how your small group is affecting your life. Share stories of how small groups have helped others in your ministry, or better yet, have them come up to the front of your group and tell their stories. If they're too shy to do that, then put it on videotape and play it. People will not get involved in small groups because they think they need to or simply because you tell them to. They'll get involved when they experience how the power of community has changed someone's life.

Secret 4: Limit your groups to same sex only. Simply put, have groups only for men and groups only for women—no coed groups. I (Ken) have some people who really disagree with me on this, but my reason is simple.

I want our small groups at Frontline to be safe places where people can be real and talk about what's going on in their lives. In a coed group, everyone wears a mask and wants to put their best foot forward; it doesn't lend itself to getting real. We do have coed groups for young married couples. However, many of these groups break out every other week, women with women and men with men. Yes, people reacted negatively to this method early on, but we've stuck to our guns now for over eight years, and it's worked.

Secret 5: Know your geographic culture. One of the reasons small groups have worked so well at Frontline is due to Washington, D.C. culture. In Washington, there's a collection of people from all over the world. Young adults come to D.C. to pad resumes, get job experience, and work on Capitol Hill as interns. As a result, D.C. is very transient.

We did a survey at Frontline a couple of years ago and found that the average Frontliner stays fourteen months and then moves out of the area. This type of culture lends itself to small groups. When people move here, they don't know anybody; and most don't have any family close by so they are very open to getting involved with small groups of Christians for prayer, study, support, and friendship.

Depending on your geographic culture, small groups might need to look a little different in order to work, but they can work if you make them a priority. Our small group ministry is the backbone of Frontline. I say that because I believe that life change happens in the context of a community where Christians are doing life together.

Your young adults will get passionate about small groups when you learn these five secrets and apply them to your life and ministry.

15. How do I teach young adults to worship?

Worship is much more than singing songs in a church service. We've defined worship more holistically as a lifestyle that focuses on glorifying God in every aspect of life. This is difficult to teach if we think of teaching as reducing worship to a body of knowledge that needs to be communicated.

Worship as a lifestyle means that I want everything I do to ultimately glorify God. A practical way this plays itself out is through decision making. If I approach any decision with the question "How will this decision glorify God?" it helps to bring clarity to the decision I need to make.

For example, if I have two equally good job offers, which job should I take? One way to boil down the pros and cons, especially for a Christian wishing to live a life of worship, is to ask: "Will either decision lend itself more to glorifying God?"

A lifestyle of worship is more caught than taught. The best way to teach worship is through one's own life example.

16. You talk a lot about creating the right environment, which seems to be characterized by a lack of condemnation. But as a discipler or a small-group leader, do I have a responsibility to God or the disciple to hold my friend accountable for lifestyle issues?

Here's how grace and truth play out in the discipleship process. God's Word is truth. This truth reveals sin in a person's life and shows them what needs to change. Yet truth alone leads to legalism and condemnation, both of which the Bible speaks against. Therefore, grace needs to be the other side of the coin.

When we talk about grace, we mean the type of relationship that helps a person embrace the truth and the things that need to be changed. Truth says, "You have sin in your life, and you need to repent and change." Grace says, "I love you unconditionally no matter what you do. I will help you and be with you as you confront the sin and repent."

People need both truth and grace to grow in Christ formation. When people experience grace, they can embrace truth.

Quest for Christ